LIFE
IN THE
TWENTIETH CENTURY

LIFE
IN THE
TWENTIETH CENTURY

AS EXPERIENCED BY
MARIE KOSS POTTER WARSAW
1916—2012

Camarillo, California

Life in the Twentieth Century

Copyright © 2000 by Marie Koss Potter Warsaw

All rights reserved under International and Pan-American Copyright Conventions.

No part of this book may be reproduced or transmitted in any form or by any means electronic or mechanical including photocopying, recording, or by any information storage and retrieval system, without written permission from the publisher, except by a reviewer, who may quote brief passages in a review. Please address inquiries to books@soulwater.org.

Printed in the United States of America

Soul Water Rising
Camarillo, California
https://soulwater.org

ISBN 978-0-9987802-5-2

First Soul Water Rising Edition, Softcover: 2021

Autobiography / Memoir / History

Cover & Interior Design: Jaiya John

PREFACE

My Autobiography

I dedicate this book to my children, grandchildren, and their descendants.

FOR SEVERAL YEARS, I had the thought that it was important for me to record the progress and history of events I have been privileged to witness and participate in during my lifetime. This thought kept recurring and with the advent of computers, I felt it was time for me to accomplish my dream. One thing kept pushing me was the desire to be able to use a computer, as I knew with that tool I could accomplish it. I felt if my grandchildren could operate a computer, I surely could learn to use one, too.

So five years ago my two sons got their heads together and ordered a computer with all the amenities they felt important for me to have. Of course with the speedy development of all kinds of new programs, it wasn't long until I ran out of memory, computer memory, I mean. I shipped my computer to Jerry, my son, and he put in seven gigabytes of memory in my computer. He assures me that should take care of anything I may want to do—let's hope so.

Marie Warsaw

INTRODUCTION

MANY YEARS AGO ON A FARM in Lee County, seven miles northwest of Keokuk, Iowa on December 24, 1916, at approximately 6:00 A.M., I arrived into this world with the aid of Dr. Lee Coffey. He had stayed the night attending my mother for the arrival of her second child. Doctors then were general practitioners and usually delivered babies in their own homes. I don't know what my birth weight was, but I was a nice, healthy baby. My mother told me that as long as I had enough to eat, I was a happy baby, and that as I grew, I enjoyed laying on a blanket on the floor instead of being held. Mother and Dad named me Ethel Marie, after my two grandmothers using their middle names. They preferred to use my middle name, and I have always been known as Marie.

The information in this book will give details of my parentage, their origin and the lifestyles of that era. During my lifetime there has been great progress in all areas of life—which I think most of you will find interesting. In this autobiography, my purpose is to relate how people lived when I was little and how each family was a self-supporting enterprise, so to speak. People worked together to provide everything they needed for their own survival and always helped any other family member that was in need. They also shared with neighbors and friends. This book will display how different life was without electricity and acquaint you with many of the different appliances developed for family use in my lifetime. I wish to portray the advancement and progress of productivity using the many inventions that were developed and made available to the general public during this century. Most of the everyday drudgery that was necessary to survive has been eliminated. This way of life is probably inconceivable to the younger generation. Also I desire to describe the growth in transportation—from horse and buggy and dirt roads to four or more lanes of paved highways all over the continent and to jet plane travel, worldwide.

CONTENTS

1. FAMILY ORIGIN — 7
2. RURAL LIVING — 23
3. NEW FAMILY MEMBER — 65
4. HIGH SCHOOL — 87
5. LEAVING HOME — 103
6. STARTING A NEW LIFE — 113
7. LIFE WITH CHILDREN — 125
8. LEAVING THE NEST — 153
9. LIVING ALONE — 163
10. GOLDEN YEARS — 169
11. MY GRANDCHILDREN — 175
12. APPENDAGES — 191
13. SUMMARY — 193
14. GENEALOGY — 195
15. ANCESTOR PICTURES — 197
16. FAMILY PHOTOS — 200
17. HISTORICAL DOCUMENT — 203
18. ANCESTOR CHARTS — 209
19. NOTES ON HISTORY AND INVENTIONS — 221

FAMILY ORIGIN
Chapter 1

INSERTED HERE IS SOME HISTORY of my parents and my grandparents, but if you don't care for history, you can skip this part. My mother, Hazel Belle Jones, and my father, Martin John Koss, married in Keokuk, Iowa, on March 23, 1914. Both of their parents were farmers.

Anton Martin Koss, my grandfather, was born March 10,1853, in West Preisen Pomerania, Germany, and was the middle child of five. His parents were Anton Martin Koss and Eva Avon Lipkin who were both born in West Preisen Pomerania, Germany. When my grandfather was sixteen, he and his family came to the United States on a sailing vessel arriving September 10, 1869. All of the family came except the oldest son, August, who was in the Prussian army, and he came two or three years later after his term of service ended. It was told that Great Grandpa brought his family to the United States because he didn't want his other sons conscripted into the army. A brother of Great Grandma Eva Lipkin Koss, who was on the ship with the family, became ill, died, and was buried at sea. Grandpa said it took six weeks to cross the Atlantic Ocean.

The Koss family settled in Detroit, Michigan, and all stayed in that area, married, and had families there except the youngest son, John, and my grandfather,

Anton. At the age of 21, Grandpa had some kind of altercation with his dad, left Detroit to do migrant farm work, and eventually settled in the Keokuk, Iowa area.

My grandmother Koss was born in Warsaw, Illinois, April 18, 1858, the daughter of Joseph Ketterer and Kresencia Baum. Joseph was born March 10, 1826, in Bollenbach Baden, Germany, and came to the United States in 1854. Krensencia was born August 15, 1830, in Empfinger, Hohenzollern, Germany, and came to the United States in 1855. They both came by way of New Orleans and settled in Quincy, Illinois, where they met and were married July 25, 1856. The two moved to Warsaw, Illinois, where Great-Grandpa Ketterer, who was a butcher and a stone mason, built a stone house for his family, and according to my brother, Marty, the foundation was still there a few years ago. My grandmother was the oldest of ten children, including two sets of twins. Three children died in infancy.

My grandmother went to a German-American school where she learned to read and write both German and English. She was a waitress in a restaurant where my grandfather came to eat his meals. Because she could speak German, they became acquainted. I don't know how long they courted, but they married on May 4, 1880. When they went to the courthouse for their marriage license, with Grandpa's very strong German accent, his name was recorded the way it sounded to the clerk—Kurtz. They carried this spelling of their name until about 1894 when they moved to Keokuk and changed their name on their records to the correct spelling, Koss. They had seven children. The oldest one, a baby girl, died in childbirth, and the two youngest boys died by the age of four. Surviving were three older girls and my father. He was born October 17, 1888, in a log cabin on a farm near

Charleston, Iowa. The family moved from there to a farm in Montrose, Iowa, and lived there about three or four years. Then they moved to a farm about three miles west of Keokuk, off of Johnson Street Road, where they operated their own dairy. They delivered milk and dairy products very early every morning to customers' homes in Keokuk. Milk was delivered in glass bottles. The empty ones were collected from the customers, taken home, washed by hand, sterilized, and refilled the following morning. These bottles were capped with purchased cardboard disks which fit in the top of the bottles.

During the winter, the children attended Catholic school in Keokuk. My dad went through the third grade. He learned arithmetic, but his teacher, a nun, read to the class instead of teaching the pupils to read. His reading skills were not developed as they should have been, and after third grade, Dad didn't want to go to school anymore and quit. Children were not forced to go to school, and the family needed Dad to help with the dairy, so they didn't object. The family all worked very hard together, which was important for their survival.

When they sold the dairy, the family bought a 40 acre farm about seven miles farther west on Johnson Street Road. This is the only home I remember, and they lived there until Grandpa Koss died in 1934. The farm had a house with seven rooms and a large screened-in side porch plus many out buildings. The large barn had an animal shelter on one side and a large hayloft in the center where hay was stored to feed the animals in the winter. Other buildings were a granary, a corn crib, and a blacksmith shop. This was used for welding, shaping farm tools, and to repair their farm machinery.

Every year the family hired a threshing machine service to thresh the wheat for storage in the granary.

When the threshing was in progress, many of the neighbor farmers came to help with the work. The women of our family and some neighbor women cooked and served dinner to all the people helping. Even with everyone working together, cooking and serving a dinner for that many people was a big project and referred to as "*Cooking for Threshers.*"

The family enjoys telling this story. After the men ate their dinner and were eating their dessert, Aunt Lena asked one of them, "Jake, would you like another piece of pie?"

Jake very indignantly answered, "I ain't had my first piece yet!"

All the men continued to help each other, and the women helped with the cooking until all the farmers had their grain threshed and stored for the winter.

Grandpa grew corn on his 40 acres which he husked by hand and tossed into the farm wagon being pulled by a team of horses. Grandpa walked with a cane and in later years used a crutch; apparently he had rheumatism in his right hip. Rheumatism was an affliction many people had and a malady doctors didn't seem to know how to treat or even help. (They still don't.) People were always figuring out some kind of treatment to ease the aching, and someone sold Grandpa a box about the size of a battery, (I guess it did contain a battery), with two cords attached to it with metal handles. A metal handle was grasped by each hand, and a little switch was turned on, giving the person holding the handles a shocking sensation through his body. This didn't cure Grandpa's rheumatism, but it probably help make the salesman rich. Grandpa could shuck more corn with his handicap than others did with two good legs. When the wagon was loaded, the corn was taken into the farm building area and stored in the corn crib. This activity was repeated until all the corn was husked. The corn stalks were tied together into shocks and left standing in the field, for what purpose I don't know, but it made a nice shelter for the birds and little wild animals through the winter.

The sides of the corn crib were built with boards spaced about an inch or so apart for ventilation which enabled the corn to dry and not mold. There was a corn sheller attached to the wall of the crib that had a crank on the side of it (to be turned by hand) for shelling the corn. We often shelled corn for Grandpa when we visited them, which seemed like most every Sunday. Today automatic drying equipment is available for drying the corn. Grandpa rented and farmed other acres of farm land on shares for his wheat. I guess farmers still do that today but with entirely different equipment—no horses (called draft animals) are used—it's all machinery now, powered by diesel or gasoline engines of various sizes depending on the equipment being used. Farm tractors[1] are used for plowing, cultivating, grading, cutting grain, or for operating various agricultural machines. The use of tractors has revolutionized agriculture.

Grandma Koss was a small lady, not quite five-feet tall. One very noticeable characteristic she had was how active she was. She never seemed to walk, but moved at such a fast pace, it was almost a run. Besides caring for her family, she took great pride in planting and caring for a large garden. In fact, she was rather competitive about it. She enjoyed harvesting produce from her garden before anyone else, like the first lettuce, first potatoes, etc. She grew enough vegetables and fruits to can and fill their cellar to last the entire winter. But her real love was flowers of all kinds. Her yard was always beautiful with pansies, tulips, lilies, daisies, asters, roses, lilacs, and many others. She enjoyed reading the many seed catalogues in the winter to find something she didn't already have. Every fall as her annual flowers went to seed, she dried and saved the seed from her best flowers to plant the next spring.

Every farm raised chickens and sometimes ducks and geese. The feathers were saved, cleaned, and made into pillows and feather beds. In the winter months, Grandma kept herself busy knitting sweaters, socks, and scarves from wool yarn for all the family. She had double-pointed steel needles, about size four, she used for all of her knitting. Since I like to knit and have become quite proficient at it, I feel proud that her needles were given to me. Grandma's favorite craft was making quilts, so Mother always saved her leftover material from her sewing for Grandma. She made many quilts in her lifetime, and as her  grandchildren married, she always had a beautiful quilt for them. We didn't realize what a treasure they would become, so we used them and wore them out. My daughter, Pamela, displays a quilt pieced by her great grandmother, Anna Koss, on her bedroom wall. It is somewhat worn, but still a treasure.

John Edward Jones, my maternal grandfather, was born November 7, 1860, in Linn County, Iowa, to Larkin Jones, born April 15, 1840, in Jefferson County, Iowa and Susan Catherine Lambert, born November 26, 1840 in Ohio. Larkin and Susan Catherine were married February 12, 1860. He was a bricklayer and an engineer.

During the Civil War, Larkin joined the 73rd regiment WMM Co T in Missouri August 5, 1862, with the rank of Corporal. He was under Captain Green's command at Lawrence Mill on active duty. They patrolled southwest Missouri and saw action in Marion County, Arkansas, December 9th to the15th, 1862, against Marmaduke. Larkin was in the service of the Union #729 for 190 days and was relieved from duty February 1863.

He again enlisted April 15, 1865. Larkin must have really felt very patriotic and dedicated to our country for him to be compelled to reenlist, instead of getting his crops planted. He mustered in on April 20, 1865, at Hannibal, Missouri, and 21 days later, died in Small Pox Hospital #456 in St. Louis, Missouri. He was buried on Small Pox Island in the Mississippi River near St. Louis. Larkin's record states, the Regiment mustered out August 31, 1865, with the loss of two enlisted men killed in service and 47 enlisted men of disease. Larkin's record named his place of residence was St. Francisville, Clark County, Missouri, occupation, engineer, at the time of his enlistment. By then he had two children, my grandfather and Amanda Jane, who died two months after her father, at the age of 20 months. (This was recorded on Larkin's service record.) Grandpa Jones was four-and-a-half years old at this time and received $8.00 a month pension from the government.

Grandpa Jones related this event he remembered, of traveling from Quincy, Illinois to St. Francisville, Missouri, with his mother and her brother, John Lambert, by horse and buggy after his father's death. A highway robber attacked them and tried to steal their horse and buggy and all their belongings. His uncle John used the hard end of the buggy whip, hitting the robber over the head, knocking him down, and leaving him lying in the road. Grandpa, being little, thought the robber was dead, but I doubt that.

Two years later in July 1867, Susan Catherine Lambert Jones married a man named William I. Howell. The following October, Howell was appointed guardian of my grandpa. In May of 1868, they had twin girls, and on January 21, 1870, Susan died, giving birth to a baby girl who also died at that time. This left my grandpa an orphan at age 10. On February 1870, Howell was relieved as guardian by court order for illegally using Grandpa's money. This was brought about by his grandfather, Morgan Jones, Jr.. He was unable to take care of Grandpa as he still had four children at home and was caring for three orphaned grandchildren of his son, William, and wife, Minerva. The court appointed Mr. Roseberry, a farmer, as guardian of Grandpa. Three years later Mr. Roseberry's wife died, and Mr. Roseberry moved away from that area.

Grandpa found a home with another farm family and worked for them until he was 17 years old. He then married, with a desire to have a home of his own. About a year later, his wife and baby daughter both died in childbirth. In February 1880, he married again and had two sons and two daughters, the youngest of which was born April 6, 1890. His wife died a few months later. Grandpa was unable to care for a wee baby, and work to support his family. His half-sister, Arrabell, who lived in Shaller, Iowa, located in the northwestern part of the state, took the baby to raise. Transportation was difficult, and the family didn't get to see the baby very often. I never knew Mother had a sister, Effie, until one time we went to Davenport, Iowa, to visit Uncle Charlie, Mother's brother. He learned Effie was living in Davenport and had been to visit her and her husband, Grant Parson. Uncle Charlie took us to visit her, and after that, we visited her occasionally.

Here is another bit of history for anyone who is interested: My brother, Marty, who has been working on genealogy for fifty years (which I'll add more information at the end of my story) learned Grandpa Jones descended from Edward III, King of England. From these descendants, records also show Grandpa Jones related to General George Washington, first president of the United States of America, and Queen Elizabeth, reigning queen of England. Another ancestor, Nicholas Marteau, from France, a Huguenot, took refuge in Belgium, then came to America on the ship *"Francis Bona Venture"* several months before the *Mayflower* left England in 1620. He settled on 1,300 acres on the York River in Virginia. (On this same land, 160 years later, his descendant, George Washington, fought and won the battle of Yorktown.)

I also have a copy of a Certificate of Election which records Grandpa Jones' election as Justice of the Peace of Clay Township, Clark County, Missouri, the 8th day of November, 1902. I do not know what all his duties entailed, but one of his duties was to perform marriages.

On October 5, 1892, Grandpa married my grandmother, Julia Ethel Pipkin, born January 5, 1872, in Keokuk, IA. She was the daughter of Mary McGlaughlin born February 9, 1841, in Hannibal, Missouri and Robert D. Pipkin born June 20, 1831 in Madison County, Tennessee. Our Pipkin ancestors (from England) settled in Virginia in early 1700, and later some migrated westward through Virginia, Tennessee, and Missouri, traveling north to Keokuk, Iowa. Grandmother Jones's grandmother, Sarah Mardis, (my great-great-grandmother) was born in Pennsylvania. In my brother's research, he discovered a letter written in 1818. The letter stated the family in Pennsylvania never knew what became of Sarah. She had married John McGlaughlin and had moves west. In those days, when people moved, their family often never knew where they went or what became of them. Enough of history. I didn't intend to write so much about it, but discovered there was a lot involved that might interest some of you.

I was told my grandmother took care of Grandpa's three other children as if they were her own. They didn't get the youngest one back, because Aunt Bell, as she was called, didn't want to give her up, even though she had many children of her own. Grandma and Grandpa had 10 more children. My mother, Hazel Bell Jones, born October 25, 1897, was the third child of that union. Two daughters died in their first year of life, and another daughter, at the age of 19. The youngest child Eunice Kronmiller who lived in Fort Wayne, Indiana, recently died at the age of 84. In September 1997, she had complications following emergency surgery. She was the last surviving sibling of that large family. Eunice was three and a half years older than I, and we grew up together. Once when I was visiting her, she introduced me to her friends as her niece and then explained to everyone that we were children together—which was true.

    My Jones grandparents did a different kind of farming. They had some acreage of their own, but also rented acreage. Grandpa Jones did what they called truck farming. This did not involve trucks as we know them today. Hardly anyone had a car then. Truck farming consisted of growing vegetables and fruits, taking them into town with a team of horses hitched to a wagon (called trucking), and selling the produce to grocery stores. Grandpa had a big umbrella over the seat for shade. Several summers, Eunice came to our house for a

week, and at the same time I visited my grandparents for a week. A couple of times when I was visiting, Grandpa took me with him. At the time it was hot and tiring, because I had to wait in the wagon at each store while Grandpa sold his produce, but I'm glad he let me go with him so that I understood what he did.

Mother told me since her folks sold the better produce, this left all the small potatoes for home use. Before she was married, it was her job to peel enough (tiny) potatoes for their large family of mostly hungry boys. The whole family worked in the fields planting, weeding, and harvesting the crops during the spring, summer, and fall Grandma worked along with Grandpa in the fields helping to have a good crop to harvest and sell. She did all this in addition to caring for her big family.

Both my grandparents' families lived in Lee County, Iowa, and even though they owned some acreage, they rented more acres in the bottom lands near the Des Moines River for farming. Being acquainted with my mother's brothers, one day my dad came to my mother's home to borrow a shovel. My mother told me her brothers kidded her about it as they had an idea Dad was more interested in my mother than he was in borrowing a shovel.

As in all rural areas, different social events were held at the local rural schoolhouse. One social event was called a *"Box Supper."* The single girls decorated a shoebox with crepe paper, lace doilies, and flowers, and filled the box with a dinner for two. These boxes were auctioned off to the male singles, and the male who bid the highest got the box and shared the dinner with the one who had prepared it. One of these events my mother participated in, resulted in my dad placing the highest bid and getting her box to share with her. The story later told was, my dad asked her brothers which one was her box, as he wanted to be the one who got it—so it was really a "set-up" for my mother.

After their marriage on March 19, 1914, they lived with my father's parents until fall, and then rented a nearby farm, known as the Howell Place, where they lived three years. My brother, Martin Ernest, was born there, March 23, 1915, and I was born there 21 months later.

Sometime before I was born, Dad had a sawmill built on a wagon frame and operated by a gasoline engine. He used it to cut logs into rough sawn lumber for building sheds on the farm and to saw up felled trees to be split for firewood for his family. (Now chain saws are used.) Sometimes other people hired Dad to saw up their felled trees into lumber. Since the sawmill was on wheels, it could be transported by horses to the farmer's land and used there. Once Dad used his right foot to scrape away some of the sawdust under the saw while the saw blade was running (a real no-no!). The saw caught his pant leg and cut a deep gash in the calf of his right leg. He was taken to the hospital where the wound was sutured and he was kept in there until it healed. It's a miracle he didn't have any trouble with infection afterward. When I was in nurse's training, Dad showed me the scar he had from the accident. (I had not known about that event before then.)

While they lived on the Howell Place, Mother was friendly with an elderly Swedish neighbor. The neighbor had a niece who wrote letters to her, but she was unable to read English. So when a letter came in the mail, she always brought it to Mother to read for her. Then Mother wrote an answering letter, her neighbor friend dictated, to send back to her niece. One day while the Swedish lady was at Mother's, a neighboring man was walking down the road and the dogs were having a real field day barking at him. The little lady retorted, "Oh, dot Palmer, he is a rascal, efan the dogs don't like him". Mother enjoyed relating this story with an accent to us when we were older.

In February following my birth, my parents had a farm sale of all their livestock and farm machinery. My father had a lot of mechanical ability and was interested in machinery, although he really was a farmer at heart. Automobiles were being touted as the coming thing, and Dad decided to go to St. Louis to study automotive repair. After three or four weeks, he came back home. He didn't like being away from his family and not being home to help, since there was always so much work to do.

We then moved to a house near Galland, Iowa, a wide spot in the road out in the country north of Keokuk, high on the bluff overlooking the Mississippi River. Dad worked in a rock quarry nearby. In those days, there were no special baby seats designed for infants, so my mother sat me on the floor in a horse collar. It was just right to support me until I was able to sit by myself. A horse collar is a large, thick, padded leather circle that fits around the horse's neck and cushions the neck of the horse when it is hitched up to pull a farm implement, wagon or buggy.

My brother, Marty, was quite inquisitive and adventurous. One day, when he was about three, he found his way to the dynamite shed for the quarry. His dog was always with him, and my folks found them both there. That was very scary for my parents. Another time, Martin Ernest was walking down the road with his dog when Dad came along in the buggy and picked them up, taking them with him on his errand. They were gone quite some time, and Mother was wild with worry because she couldn't find Martin Ernest. I'm sure my dad never took him again without telling her!

Later we moved from that area into Keokuk where Dad worked for the Union Carbide. Mother told me I was one-and-a-half and Marty was three when the three of us became sick with scarlet fever. We were quarantined—which meant no one was allowed to come into the house. Dad had to work and could only come as far as the door to see what Mother needed and to get it for us. Even though she was sick, she had to care for us, and she said she didn't know how any of us survived.

Work wasn't steady at the Union Carbide. Dad obtained employment at E.I. Du Pont de Neumoir & Co. where he had worked at one time before they were married. He continued to work there many years, making dynamite used in mines and quarries. One might say he had a *"dynamic"* job. My brother, Marty, tells me black blasting powder was made there, not dynamite. Oh well, I don't know the difference as they are both dangerous explosives. Apparently, the composition of the two are different.

Du Pont Co. owned over a thousand acres of hilly wooded land about seven miles north of Keokuk where they built their plant. As a safety precaution, the buildings were scattered throughout the hills so that no building was close to another. On rare occasions when one of the mills blew up, no other mill was affected. The plant was surrounded by a high wire fence topped with barbed wire and *"No Trespassing"* signs posted all along the top.

Houses were built for the employees away from the plant on two different sites called settlements with a man-made lake between. I was about three when Dad went to work there and we moved into one of the houses. It was a small four room-house where we lived about a year.

Then my parents bought a small eight-acre farm about two miles from the plant, (earlier, I stated Dad was always a farmer at heart), where we lived about four years. I have vague memories of some of the other places we lived earlier, but this is the one I really remember. Dad either walked or rode a horse to work. Our family's mode of transportation was a horse and buggy. The country roads were not graveled or paved—just clay—very dusty in the summer when dry, very slippery when wet, and the clay stuck to your shoes like glue. I remember how the clay stuck to the buggy wheels, wrapping around them in a wide sheet, which caused my parents to stop ever so often and scrape it off. One of my jobs was cleaning Dad's good shoes whenever he got mud on them. It was important not to have dried mud on your shoes or clothes when we went someplace.

    While we lived there, Dad had an appendicitis attack that required an operation. In those days recuperation from this kind of surgery required a hospital stay of three weeks. It is much different today. I think that kind of surgery is done on an outpatient basis now unless the appendix has ruptured.

RURAL LIVING

Chapter 2

LIVING IN A RURAL AREA meant there was no electricity, modern conveniences, or indoor plumbing. Water was pumped from a cistern into a water bucket, brought into the house, and placed on a wash bench for use in cooking and for washing. The bucket held a long handled-ladle used for dipping the water and for 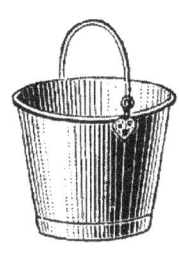 drinking. Beside the bucket was a wash basin in which we washed our face and hands. After the water was used, it was thrown outside on the grass.

    Our toilet facility was at the end of an approximately 100 foot path. This was known as an *"Outhouse,"* a small building about five-foot square built  over a hole in the ground. A closed bench was built against the back wall with two holes in the top for seating purposes. All rural homes received catalogues from mail-order houses, like Sears & Roebuck and Montgomery Wards. They were our department stores. (Of course, we shopped in Keokuk for many things as it was a nice size town.) Each year, the companies sent new catalogues, and the old ones were used for toilet paper. Powdered lime was put into the bottom of the toilet to help eliminate some of the odor. I never thought it helped much. The "Outhouse" was very hot in the summer and very cold in the winter. I might add, it wasn't used as a reading room.

Our home was heated by two wood-burning stoves that Dad provided wood for. Every year, he chopped down trees, sawed them up, and split the big logs. My brother and I had the chore of stacking the wood in the woodshed. The living room was heated by a potbellied stove which was stored in a shed in the summer. One winter evening, Mother wasn't feeling well and seemed to be chilling. So Dad added more wood to the stove, and the fire became so hot that the outside of the chimney wall above the stove burst into flames. That was very frightening! Dad ran to the kitchen and grabbed the pail of water. He threw the water up on the wall and put out the fire. (What a close call.)

In the kitchen, we had a cookstove or range that was used all year. My brother's chore was to fill the wood bin in the living room with the bigger logs in the winter. I had the chore of always filling the wood box in the kitchen with split wood and kindling to be used in the cookstove. On the left end of the cookstove was a firebox, and under it, a container to catch the ashes. On the right side next to this was the oven, and at the right end of the stove was a container to hold water, called a reservoir. Over all this was the stove top where pots and pans were placed to cook the food. The area over the firebox was the hottest and was used for quick cooking, the next area was used for slower cooking, and the right end was for keeping the food warm. So Mother placed the pots on the area that was best suited for what she was cooking. The reservoir was kept full of water to insure warm water was always available for use. Across the back of the range was a back splash upon which two small warming ovens about two feet above the cooking area were fastened. (A stove that could do anything but microwave.)

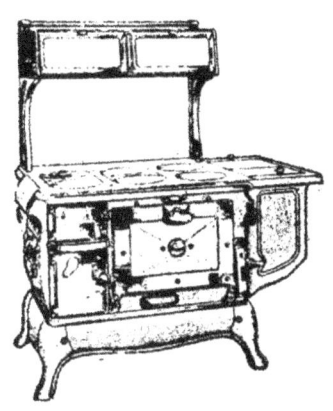

My mother was a very good cook baking delicious pies and cakes from scratch. Anything ready mixed was unheard of then. A joke making the circles today is "A new bride was having trouble cooking for her husband. It seemed nothing was as good as his mother made it, and she decided to talk with her mother-in-law to learn how she prepared his food. Her mother-in-law's answer was she made everything from scratch. The bride went shopping but was unsuccessful in finding any product called scratch. After asking the store manager if he knew where she could buy it, he explained to her what scratch meant." I remember, when I was a new bride, asking my mother-in-law directions for making something that Harold liked, and her telling me how by saying, "Well, you put a little pinch of this and a small portion of that in." I had to request just how much all that was by measurement. I wasn't good at *"little pinches"* and *"small portions."* My mother's oven had no automatic controls, but she knew just how much fuel was needed for a specific purpose. Eventually small kerosene three-burner stoves were available, and we were able to purchase one to use in the summer for cooking. It made a hot job much cooler!

The dirty dishes were washed by placing two large dish pans on the table, one for washing the dishes in hot, soapy water and the other for stacking the dishes in to be rinsed. Boiling water was poured over the dishes to sterilize them, and then dried with a dish towel. If someone helped with the dishes, hot water was put in the pan and the dishes dipped into it before drying them. This helped to prevent germs being passed on to everyone else in the family when someone had a cold.

Laundry was done <u>manually</u> in the kitchen. By manually, I mean two wash tubs were placed on a bench, one for washing and the other for rinsing the clothes. Water for washing the clothes was heated on the cookstove. If you see a thing in a museum called a washboard made of corrugated metal in a wooden frame, this is what was used to scrub the clothes on. A bar  of soap was rubbed onto the soiled clothes, then rubbed over the washboard many times. Some people wrung the clothes out by hand and then rinsed them in the other tub filled with clear water. But my mother had a wringer composed of two rollers with gears on each end and fastened by clamps to one of the tubs. The gears meshed together when turned by a hand crank. When I was big enough, it was my job to turn the wringer as Mother fed the clothes between the hard rubber rollers.

Later we had a washing machine with wringer attached. It was constructed of a round wooden tub on four legs. Inside the tub was a fixture with four pegs attached, which agitated the clothes. This was accomplished by a handle on the outside of the tub being pulled back and forth by hand to operate the fixture. My brother, who had this job, told me that for every load of clothes washed, the handle had to be pulled 100 times. If Marty finished too quickly, Mother seemed to know and would tell him he hadn't done it enough. It wasn't his favorite chore. However this was quite an improvement from having to lean over a washtub to scrub the clothes by hand on a washboard. My mother boiled the white clothes with soap and water in a copper boiler on top of the cookstove. This made the clothes nice and white. (I still have the boiler; only I put fireplace wood in it. The copper boilers have become a collector's item.)

The clothes were hung up to dry outside on a wire clothesline. Although the wire was made of steel and wouldn't rust, it had to be wiped clean before used to prevent black marks on the clothes. When the clothes were dry, they were brought back into the house. Towels and rags use for cleaning were folded and put away. The rest of the clothes were sprinkled with water, rolled up to even the dampness, then ironed the next day. How? With something called flat irons (you can see these in museums, too) heated on the cookstove—even in summer. It was good to have about four irons, because as one was used and it cooled off, it was taken back to the stove to reheat, and another one was used. These irons had a detachable handle that had a wood holder on the top. Old-fashioned irons had metal handles built right on them, so a pad or potholder was needed to hold them while in use. (The handle was as hot as the iron.) I don't remember Mother having that kind, but both my grandmothers did. Today, people like to use them for doorstops. Wash-and-wear material was not created yet; everything was made from cotton, linen, silk, rayon, or wool, and had to be ironed. Even the sheets and pillowcases were always ironed.

A new type of iron became available. This iron was designed with a small gasoline tank pressurized by a little pump and fastened onto the end of the handle. The flow of gasoline was adjusted to keep the iron at a certain temperature. Mother bought one of them and found it a great improvement over the flat irons that were heated on the stove. It was called a gasoline iron and worked very well, but was dangerous. Even though Mother was very careful when using it, I was afraid of it and never did use it.

The *Peoria Journal Star* paper had an article the other day dealing with question and answers about antiques, quote:

"Q: I have a strange looking pressing iron that has a round ball at the back. It seems like it would hold some sort of fuel. When were irons made that did not have electric cords?

A: The first irons were just heavy pieces of metal, usually iron, that could be heated on a stove. Early 19th century attempts were made using whale oil to heat the iron. It was an expensive fuel. Later, many types of fueled irons were tried. Some used kerosene, some gasoline and others naphtha. Each could explode if mishandled. Because of the danger, the ironing board usually was kept near a door. In case of fire, the iron was thrown outside the house. A fueled iron needed a tank. Some held the fuel on the side or under the handle. Self-heating irons were popular in rural America until the 1930s, because only a small percentage of the farmhouses had electricity. Most makers stop making fueled irons by the 1950s."

Ironing boards were usually made from a board tapered on one end, padded with an old blanket, covered with an old sheet, and supported by placing it across the back of two kitchen chairs. Some people laid the board on their kitchen table to use.

Both my grandmothers made their own soap with grease they collected from cooking, lye, and wood ash. This was all mixed together in a large iron kettle and cooked over an open fire outside. After cooking this mixture the required time, it was poured into flat containers. The soap was allowed to set up and become firm, and then cut into bars and dried. Synthetic detergents[2] had not been developed yet. Until the 1940s, soap was the only important cleansing agent.

Rainwater was collected in cisterns from down spouts off the roof or into rain barrels if there was no cistern (most homes had cisterns). The rainwater was used for all tasks, when available, as the soap could be rinsed out better. There were no minerals in the water to merge with the soap, causing the suds to curdle. A cistern was built by digging a hole about 12 feet deep, six-feet in diameter, and lined with bricks. To keep the cistern water fresh, it needed to be emptied and scrubbed every few years.

Some of our neighbors did not do all of this work to be clean, and their homes were very dirty. We had two such families in our area, and I never enjoyed going there.

About baths—every Saturday evening, Mother put a round metal wash tub about 36 inches in diameter in the middle of the kitchen floor. She put water in the tub for Marty and me to bathe in, whether we needed it or not. I was given my bath first, then my brother, in the same water. When we were little, we fit in that tub fairly well, but as we got older, it wasn't as easy. But we were nice and clean for the week, and the next day, we went by horse and buggy into Keokuk to Sunday school and church at the First Baptist Church. Mom and Dad sat on the seat, and my brother and I sat backwards on a board placed across the inside of the front of the buggy against the dashboard. When the horse swished his old tail, it hit us in the back of the head and sometimes hit us across the face. That really stung! In the wintertime, Mother heated bricks for our feet and covered us with a heavy wool lap robe to keep us warm.

In the summertime, we went barefooted when we were home. Mother had a small tub about half the size of the laundry tub (like a miniature washtub) called a foot tub. Every night before we went to bed, we had to go out on the back stoop and sit on the step to wash our feet in the foot tub. Mother wouldn't allow us to go to bed with dirty feet.

When I was about four years old, my brother and I were playing in our yard. He was pulling the push lawnmower upside-down, making the blades go around. I was holding onto the roller that helped the pushing of the mower when it was in its regular position. I guess I lost my balance, and the end of my right thumb caught in the lawnmower  blade. The end of my thumb and part of my thumb nail was cut quite badly. Mother took me by horse and buggy to a doctor in Keokuk, an old-fashioned general practitioner. He cleaned it, put some special salve on it, and sent some home so Mother could change the dressing. It healed up without any complications except I still have a scar. But I still marvel that I didn't get tetanus.

In later years, small gasoline engines designed to operate lawnmowers with a whirling blade revolutionized the care of lawns. Later small riding tractors using the same type of blade have become a very popular appliance for mowing lawns. However, the other power mower is still necessary for trimming edges. Other types of trimmers have been designed but never proved successful.

My brother and I were called Sonny and Sissy when we were little, but when I was five and started to school, we were instructed to call each other by our given names. Since my Dad's name was Martin, I had to learn to call Marty by his full name *"Martin Ernest"*. This was quite a change. If I forgot to use his full name, I was scolded by Dad (and he didn't scold gently).

The school we attended was about a mile from our home. The first class was called primary where we were taught phonics and numbers. After a couple of months, if a student was able to do the work, the pupil was promoted into first grade. If not, he or she was kept in primary the rest of the year. I was promoted into first grade my first year at school. Most

rural schools had only one room with eight grades, but since there were more students in this area because of the Du Pont Settlement, there was a need for two rooms with four grades taught in each. This building was

different from other country school buildings as there was a full basement under it. We used this at recess and lunch when the weather was too bad to be outside. About 20 to 25 pupils were in each room. School was in session the same as it is today— from September to June. We walked to and from school (no buses) and carried our lunches in a lunch bucket. Some children used a half-gallon syrup pail, which had a wire bail for a handle. Our lunch buckets were like the metal lunch buckets you can buy today but had no thermos bottles. We had a 15 minute recess mid-morning and mid-afternoon for playing outside and using the "necessary little out building". We had an hour for lunch, and after we ate, we had time to play on slides, swings, teeter- totters, and games supervised by our teacher, like *Drop the Handkerchief, Who Has the Ball, Simon Says*, etc. The older children played *baseball*. In the winter, if we couldn't go outside to play, we sometimes played *musical chairs* with the teacher playing a record on the victrola.

A coat room was just off the entrance hall of the school for our coats and overshoes as the weather got colder. Our school room was heated by a wood burning potbellied stove in the back of each room. One of the teacher's duties was to keep the fire burning during cold weather. For my second year of school, our parents changed my brother and me to another school, which was a one-room school. Since we lived about halfway between the two schools, we had a choice of which one we wanted to attend. Our parents decided to change us because the older boys attending the other school were mean to the smaller ones. But the main influence was Gardener school had a better teacher, named Hazel Vieth. She lived on the main road to Keokuk and went past our home in her horse and buggy to the schoolhouse. This was nice because she often picked Marty and me up to take us to school with her.

During cold weather, we wore long knitted cotton underwear. It was a one-piece garment buttoned down the front with long legs and long sleeves with a buttoned drop-down flap in the back for necessary bodily functions. We wore long black cotton stockings over our underwear and black laced-up shoes that covered our ankles. When there was snow, we wore overshoes made of rubber fastened with four buckles that fit over our shoes. I always wore printed cotton dresses my mother made for me. Girls didn't wear overalls or slacks, and the boys always dressed in bib overalls. In the winter we wore sweaters, heavy coats, scarves, stocking caps, and gloves or mittens. As I mentioned before, we almost always walked to school.

We became friends with one of our neighbors and often went to Keokuk together for a shopping day. Mother hitched our horse to our buggy and took Mrs. Kennedy and her younger daughter shopping mostly for grocery staples, such as flour, sugar, cereal, rice, and things of that nature. Mother left our horse and buggy in front of the home of Aunt Em who lived close to downtown. One time it appeared someone had borrowed our horse and buggy as it was placed in a different position when we went back to it. As we were driving back to the country, our horse was very jittery and difficult for Mother to control. This made Mrs. Kennedy very nervous. Mother finally got the horse to stop, and Mrs. Kennedy, Bernice, and I got out of the buggy and started walking. I couldn't understand why we were walking. I knew we could never walk all the way home. Mother turned our buggy around and went back to town, trying to settle the horse down. A little while later, she returned and picked us back up. The horse was apparently all right the rest of the way home. (Mother probably gave him a lecture.)

One day when Mother was driving the horse and buggy along the road to town (we must have been in school), something scared the horse. He shied and overturned the buggy in the gutter on the side of the road. Mother wasn't hurt, only shaken up and scared. However, someone came along and helped her set the buggy upright, so she went on into town to do the errands she had planned for the day. Fortunately, she didn't have the neighbors or us with her on that trip.

Mother never cooked rice as a main dish but used it to make rice pudding, Marty's favorite dessert. She also made tapioca pudding, a favorite of the whole family. What I liked most was Mother's egg custard and also her bread pudding made with egg custard. We didn't buy canned goods because Dad and Mother grew our food in our garden and Mother canned it. We also had fruit trees and all kind of berries which Mother canned.

Most farmers were poor, but living on a farm had advantages people in the city didn't have. My family grew most of their own food and preserved it for winter. In the winter they butchered a cow and a pig, and canned the meat. The fat from the pig was rendered

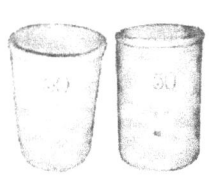

into lard for cooking by cutting the fat from the meat into small cubes. The fat was put into a large black iron kettle that had small legs and hung from a tripod in the yard with a fire built under the kettle. The fat had to be stirred frequently so it did not burn (that would spoil the flavor of the lard). The lard was dipped out of the kettle and put into 20 gallon crock jars. These were covered carefully and stored in the cellar under the house. The trimmings from the meat were ground up by a large meat grinder attached on a board. Of course, the meat grinder had a handle that had to be turned by hand. Sausage was made from this and canned for later use. Grandma Koss had a sausage stuffer that she used to fill casings with the ground meat. That's the way the Germans did it. Dad's cousin, Johnny Ketterer, had a meat market in Keokuk for many years, and his specialties were wieners and bologna sausage. They were a real treat—nothing like the ones sold in stores today. After I was grown and married, we often brought home some of Johnny's wieners when we went to Keokuk to visit my family.

Bacon and ham were smoked in a smokehouse. We didn't have a smokehouse, but Dad's parents had one we used. When you went into the smokehouse, it had a very distinct smell of its own; there is no other odor quite like it. It was an aroma that made you hungry for some of the ham or bacon that was cured there.

Canning was a detailed process. Mother put the food into clean canning jars and sealed them with a jar rubber and lid, being careful to keep the rubber or jar lid free from any food that would let mold into the jar and spoil the food. Preserving vegetables required placing the filled jars with the lid not quite tight into a large container on the stove. Mother used her boiler for this task. A wire rack was used to keep the jars spaced and off the bottom of the boiler. The jars were covered with water, and the water was brought to a boil and kept boiling for three hours on the cookstove. This sterilized the food so it wouldn't spoil, and when the jars were removed from the water, the lids were tightened immediately and placed on the cabinet upside-down to seal and cool. This was a hot job for summer.

Fruit could be done the same way, except it didn't have to be boiled as long, just 30 minutes. This method of canning was called cold packing. But there was another method used to can fruit and also tomatoes, called open kettle canning. The fruit was peeled and prepared for canning. Enough fruit to fill two, or three, quart jars was placed in a kettle with sugar water and brought to a full boil. Jars and lids had been washed clean, and a couple of jars at a time were placed into a pan of boiling water to sterilize them. Cooked fruit was put into a jar, the top wiped clean, and a rubber ring and jar lid that had also been sterilized in boiling water was put on and tightened.

Beside fruits and vegetables, all types of food were canned for winter, including pickles, catsup, chili sauce (or salsa as it is called today), corn relish, pickled beats, spiced peaches, and spiced pears. Juice from all kinds of fruit was made into jelly, and a variety of fruits were used to make preserves. Strawberry and plum preserves were my favorites. All of this food was stored on shelves in a cellar under the house—like a small unfinished one-room basement with a dirt floor. Potatoes, carrots, onions, and other root vegetables were also stored in the cellar. I always say, I didn't know we were poor, since we were never cold or hungry. As I look back on it, I still don't think we were poor.

When I was about five years old, my folks purchased a Model-T Ford automobile. It was a touring car that had two leather seats wide enough for two people on each. It had detachable curtains with isinglass (definition—mica, chiefly in the form of thin sheets) in the center of  them for visibility. These curtains were fastened into place by little metal buttons attached to the automobile. The buttons slid through small holes placed around the edge of the curtains, and were turned to lock the curtains in place when it rained or was cold. The car was not a new one, but we thought it was great. To start the engine, Dad or Mother had to turn a crank that fit into the front of the engine. It was no easy trick because the gas lever attached to the steering wheel post had to be adjusted just so. On the other side of the steering wheel post was a spark lever that helped the car start and had to be adjusted just right also. When the engine started after turning the crank, my parent had to run quickly to the steering wheel to readjust the spark and gas levers. Sometimes when cranking the engine, the crank would kick backwards, causing a sprained wrist or even a broken arm, so they were always careful. Mother taught herself to drive the car, and then we didn't have to use the horse and buggy anymore.

One day Mother was in the barn milking *Old Blackie*, our cow, when *Smarty*, our rooster, flew up and landed on the horn that was attached to the side of the car. This made the horn toot, causing the rooster to jump up and land on the horn again making the horn sound again and again, "Uga, Uga" (pronounced with a long U).

Mother thought Martin Ernest was tooting the horn and called him to stop it, but he was nowhere near the car. Oftentimes we tooted the horn just to hear it make that funny noise, so she wasn't too wrong in thinking it was one of us.

Autos didn't travel too well on the dirt roads when it rained. My brother, Marty, remembered this story. The funeral parlor in Keokuk had a motor vehicle they could use as an ambulance, and they were called to pick up someone sick who lived beyond us on the Argyle Road (the road past by our house). It had rained, and as the ambulance was going up the small hill of slick clay beside our home, it slid into the ditch. A team of horses was brought and attached to the car but was unable to pull it out of the ditch. The sick person was loaded onto a lumber wagon and taken to the hospital in Keokuk. We never knew how sick he was or if he survived. They finally removed the ambulance from the ditch by using the team of horses and a big heavy block and tackle, which they tied onto our big apple tree.

Dad's sister, Aunt Lena, and her family lived on an 80 acre farm about two miles from us. Aunt Lena's husband, who had been sick for a long time with a very bad heart, died at Easter time of my second year of school. Aunt Lena and her family couldn't take care of the farm and wanted to move into Keokuk. Dad and Mother sold our little eight-acre farm, bought the one Aunt Lena had, and we moved there. My brother and I didn't change schools as the farm was less than a mile on the other side of the school we were attending. That was better because we didn't have as far to walk to school.

We still attended Sunday school and church in Keokuk. On April 17, 1925, my dad, brother and I were baptized by immersion in the Baptist Font situated behind the pulpit in the First Baptist Church in Keokuk, Iowa.

Dad had learned enough about automobiles that he was able to fix our car when something was out of adjustment, or the spark plugs needed to be cleaned or replaced. There were four "things" about the size of bricks (but not of brick material) that fit in a box attached inside the car under the windshield and were called coils. If water leaked on them and they became wet, the car would not start. When this happened, the coils were taken into the house to dry out. This always remained a puzzle to me; I did not understand it.

After we moved to the new farm, we had to cross a bridge over a small creek followed by a very steep hill. The hill wasn't real long, but our car apparently lost power and had difficulty making it up this hill. The car still seemed to have power going in reverse, and one day when Mother couldn't make it up the hill, she turned the car around and backed up the hill. I was about eight and my cousin, Mae, was with us, and I remember how frightened she was. After that, Dad worked on the car. He took the engine out with a block and tackle, put new rings in the pistons, then put it back together. (I didn't think it would ever run again, but it did.) This fixed the engine problem and we never had any more trouble with it.

We often had flat tires, and if this happened when we were going some place without Dad, Mother was able to jack up the wheel, remove the tire, patch the inner tube, and put it all back together. Away we went again! Once they bought solid rubber tires that couldn't be punctured. I thought this was a great idea, but the tires didn't work very well because the car bounced on the road too much. This made the car harder to control, and the tires were soon replaced. Bear in mind, none of the roads were paved or graveled—just dusty dirt, and after a rain, sticky, slippery clay. During the spring thaw after the freezing winter, there usually was an area where the *"bottom would go out of the road"* as it was expressed. This created a big mud hole where people got stuck, including us. Dad went to a nearby farmer who hitched up a team of horses and pulled us out. Thinking about it now, the humor of the situation was the automobile still had to depend on horses. All the farmers knew each other. It was not like asking a stranger to help, and they always helped when anyone had a problem; but I think Dad gave him some money for his trouble. When I go back to that area now, it is strange to see all the roads widened and black-topped.

Following is a copy of an article printed in the Peoria Journal paper June 1996:

AMERICAN CAR INDUSTRY PASSES THE CENTURY MARK

Detroit {AP} America's love affair with the automobile was born shortly after the Duryea brothers built and sold thirteen identical gas-powered motor wagons a century ago in Massachusetts and later in Peoria. This weekend, centennial celebrations in Michigan feature thousands of antique and classic cars, and on Sunday, *Tonight Show* host, Jay Leno, will

serve as the grand marshal of the National Auto 100 Parade. In 1896, Charles and J. Frank Duryea of Springfield, Massachusetts, produced the 13 Duryea Motor-Wagons, marking the first time more than one vehicle was manufactured from the same design. They later set up shop in Peoria. But it was Henry Ford who took the idea of a production car a step further. Ford had a plan to produce affordable cars for the masses and to improve assembly line methods to cut production costs. The cars changed the form of rural America, taking people from the farm to the city and making it possible to decide where you wanted to go and when.

The production manufacturing of these autowagons began just 20 years before I was born. I believe this article gives a clear picture of the beginning of the automobile age. Not very many people had cars, and the roads were not quickly improved for car usage. The design of the first cars was high off the ground, and a running board was needed on each side of the car to step up onto to get into the car. As the speed of the car increased, accidents began to occur. The roads had 90-degree angled corners where many of the accidents happened, and these corners were eventually replaced with curves to enable the automobile to negotiate the turns better. The design of automobiles was also changed, Instead of looking so much like a buggy, they had smaller wheels and built lower to the ground making them safer. Miraculous advancements in traveling have occurred through the years of my life, from two-lane clay roads to four; six; and sometimes eight-lane super highways.

  We were disappointed to learned our teacher, Miss Vieth, was transferring to another school, and our school needed to find a replacement for her. In rural areas, it was necessary for the school teacher to find a place to board if she was not from that area. Our new teacher was from a small town somewhat distant from our school. She approached our family requesting my parents to let her board with us. My parents decided it could be arranged for her to stay with us. Although our home was not too big and didn't have an extra bedroom, the teacher, Miss Case, accepted the fact she would share a bed with me. Mother was very clean and a very good cook, which were two important attributes for boarding. Living fairly close to the school also made it nicer for the teacher; as she had to walk to the school like the pupils. Miss Case became just like one of the family.

One of our neighbors, a young man of courting age named Edgar Brandenburg, found Miss Case very attractive and spent a lot of evenings at our home. He lived with his parents on a farm not too far from us and often walked over to our house. By the road it was a couple of miles, but if he cut through the woods, it was much closer. One time when Edgar was going home he decided to take the shortcut. It was quite dark and there was a little creek Edgar had to cross, but he had forgotten his flashlight. You guessed it. He reached the creek before he realized it and fell in, getting soaking wet. It's a good thing he was on his way home when that happened. Another time when he came, it was Marty's birthday and tradition was to give the birthday child a spanking. As Edgar proceeded to spank Marty, our dog, Skeezix, jumped at Edgar and bit him. Marty really enjoyed that turnabout of events.

The catalogues we received every year were no doubt a big part of our education. We read about what was available in the outside world and also looked at the toys with a lot of "wishing." At Christmas time, Santa brought us one major toy, a sack of candy, and an orange. At Sunday school, we were given a small box of hard Christmas candy. One year from Santa, I received a rocking chair and the next year a doll that was called a Mama Doll. When I rocked the doll and held it in a certain position, it said *"Ma Ma."* The following year, I was given a doll bed for my doll, and the year after that, a little sewing machine, which sewed a change stitch. The machine operated by turning the wheel, with the little knob on it, positioned on the right end of the machine. I made little doll dresses out of left over material Mother gave me from pieces she made our dresses from. We kept our toys from year to year as we knew they would not be replaced. These were the Christmases that stand out in my memory over all the others.

Every Christmas, Dad's two sisters and their families, who lived in Lee County, and our family went to my paternal grandparents. It was always a festive gathering with all the family attending. Grandma took pride in serving some of everything she had preserved in her food cellar. It was a real feast! Grandma roasted chickens and also a turkey she had raised. Before Christmas, Grandma spent long hours preparing many different kind of cookies and candy to serve on this special day. My mother and two aunts fixed special dishes to take to the dinner.

My grandparents had a round oak table with six table leaves that extended the table the length of the dining room. At the end of the extended table, additional small table legs dropped down to support the ends of the table. This created space for many place settings but still was not big enough. There were too many people to serve at one time, and the children always had to wait until the adults finished eating. Then the table was reset for the younger children. I don't think it is done that way today. (I never made my children wait for a second table when we had company. I would add another table, so we could all sit down and eat together. But our gatherings weren't that big either.)

The families gathered at our home for New Year's Day dinner, and we all went to Aunt Grace's and Aunt Lena's for Thanksgiving and Easter. It seemed, we spent a lot of Sundays and holidays with my father's family. Dad's other sister, Aunt Annie, lived in Nebraska and wasn't able to come to the farm in Keokuk because of the distance. She had also suffered severe asthma attacks when she had attempted to visit. Aunt Annie was allergic to the farm animals, and this was the big reason for her family not being able to attend.

A creek with nice clean sand ran through Grandpa Koss's farm, and the younger grandchildren loved to play in the sand in the summer. There was always more sand than water in the creek and we spent many hours building farms in the sand. We liked to walk across fallen logs that spanned the creek and climb trees. It was fun to climb a tree, but difficult for me to get back down. I usually needed help. At our home in the summer, Dad tied a rope to a tire and onto a limb of a tree in our front yard for us to use as a swing. Many children had this kind of a swing.

A little note about our pets when we were small. We got the name of our small black-and-white fox terrier, Skeezix, from the funnies. A friend of great-aunt Em always saved the funny papers for us from the *Chicago Tribune*, and we looked forward to receiving the funnies. We received the *Daily Gate City* newspaper everyday, but it had no Sunday paper. I don't remember our other dog we had when I was little; he was Marty's pal. We also had several cats that kept the mice population down. They were almost too wild to play with, but when they were little we had fun with them. Grandpa Koss had a Collie dog, named Shep. Shep was trained to go out in the pasture and bring in the cows in the evening to be milked. Grandpa called to Shep, "Go get the cows," and away he ran to get them.

Many times through the year we went to our maternal grandparents on Sunday. My grandmother Jones was a very good cook. Her cooking was southern style, and although she wasn't raised in the south, history shows her family migrated west from Virginia through Kentucky, Tennessee, and north to Missouri and Iowa, settling in Keokuk. Grandma rolled cut up chicken in seasoned flour and put it in a big square pan in the oven of the cookstove. When it was brown she turned it over and browned the other side. From the drippings she made creamed gravy and served it with mashed potatoes. It makes me hungry for some now, just thinking how good it was. I especially remember her bread and how delicious it was. Grandma had a large family and baked bread three times a week. Once in a great while, she gave me a loaf of bread to take home after our visit there. <u>She couldn't give me anything I liked better</u>.

With her large family, she used the contents of a 50 pound sack of flour every week. The flour came in large white muslin sacks with black-and-red printing on the outside, stating the brand of flour and where it was made. This was a challenge to my grandmother to scrub and boil the sacks so every bit of the printing was removed. There was a reason for doing that. She used these sacks to make many articles for the home and also her undergarments—like bloomers, slips and nightgowns. For the home, she embroidered designs on them for dish towels and tablecloths. Grandma never liked to serve her family meals on a bare table. She was a beautiful seamstress, and when she made anything by hand, her stitches were very tiny. Another tedious task she performed was to clean and save feathers for making pillows and feather beds for the winter for extra warmth. We were very family-oriented and able to supply many of our own needs. Nothing was wasted.

When I was in the sixth or seventh grade, I realized it was unusual for anyone to have four living grandparents.

When I was small, Aunt Em and Uncle John lived in Nauvoo, Ilinois across the Mississippi River from Montrose Iowa. There was no bridge there, but someone operated a ferry boat, and we crossed the river on it when we went to visit them. It was much closer to us rather than going to Keokuk to use the bridge, and  it was a fun way to go, Also going 14 extra miles with a horse and buggy took a lot more time. I thought you might enjoy a picture of the boat. There was a ferry boat in operation south of Keokuk between Alexandria, Missouri and Warsaw, Illinois, and sometimes we crossed the river on it, when we wanted to visit one of Mother's brothers and his family who lived on a farm there.

Various social events were held at the school. Sometimes someone played the piano (every school had a piano), and someone played the fiddle (or violin). One of the farmers, an old German fellow (well he seemed old to me at the time), sometimes danced a jig, but he liked to be coaxed first. The women brought pies to share, and everyone enjoyed pie and coffee. Most of the children didn't drink coffee, so they just had pie. Mother was a great cook, her pies were the best, and I always hoped to get a piece of her pie.

At home in the summer, we often had homemade ice cream and cake made from scratch (there were no ready-made mixes). Mother cooked a custard to use in the ice cream as this made the ice cream nice and smooth. The ice cream was made by hand-turning an ice cream freezer. A mixture of salt and ice was put in the freezer between the container holding the solution for the ice cream and the outside part of the freezer. The reason for using salt and ice is when you mix salt, ice, and water, the temperature at which water freezes goes down. As the salt comes in contact with the ice, the ice begins to melt without changing the temperature of the water keeping it as cold as if it were ice. When the mixture on the inside of the freezer compartment comes in contact with the freezer, it is chilled to freezing. As the crank is turned, the paddle in the ice cream container scrapes the inside of the container and keeps the liquid moving so all parts of it are chilled to freeze evenly. (I really wanted to state, eventually). When we went to town, Dad and Mother bought the ice in Keokuk at the icehouse in a 100 pound chunk. They covered this with gunny sacks and newspaper to keep it from melting too much before we got home with it. My sons, remembering what a fun family affair it was to make ice cream by hand, most always make ice cream on family get-togethers. Everyone must take a turn at the crank, or they forfeit their right to eat any ice cream. <u>Everyone always takes their turn</u>! There are electric ice cream freezers now, and my parents bought and used one in their later years, but my sons don't want one. They want to adhere to the old fashioned tradition.

     Dad built an ice chest made of two wooden boxes, one smaller which fit inside the other one with sawdust packed between them for insulation. The lid was made the same way. There was a drain hole in the bottom, and the water from the ice, as it melted, drained out and soaked into the dirt floor of the cellar. This helped keep our dairy food cold in the summer when we had ice. Mother usually milked the cows; I never learned to do that.   Grandma Koss had a milk separator that separated the cream from the milk. It was a tall machine, about four-and-a-half feet, that stood in the corner of the screened-in porch of their home. A very large metal bowl for the milk was positioned on top of it. On the side of the separator was a large handle with a crank on it that was turned by hand. Some of the whole milk was set aside to use fresh. The rest of the milk was poured into the bowl of the separator, and as the crank was turned, the milk went through a series of small cone-like discs and drained out through two spouts into containers. The cream came out one spout, and the skimmed milk came out the other.

The separator discs were numbered, 50 or more, and held together by a small metal ring. Every day the separator had to be washed thoroughly and the discs put back together according to number to make it work properly. I never did understand exactly how it worked.

Some of the skimmed milk was used to make cottage cheese and for cooking, and the rest was fed to the animals. Cream was used for making butter and cooking. To make butter, cream was poured into a tall two-gallon crock that had a wooden lid with a hole in the center. A wooden paddle with a handle fit through the hole and it was moved up and down repetitively until the cream separated into butter and buttermilk. The butter was removed, salt added, and pushed into a butter mold which created a design on the top of the butter when it was removed. The  buttermilk was also used for cooking, some for drinking, and the rest fed to the hogs. Nothing ever went to waste. I never liked buttermilk, but many people did. I learned butter could be made another way. Our neighbor put cream into a quart jar with the lid tightened and chilled the cream by hanging the jar in the cistern. Then the jar was held with one hand on top and the other hand on the bottom and shaken back and forth until the butter separated from the milk. I didn't think this was such a good method since it seemed to take a long time. It was easier to use a regular churn.

Eventually a glass churn became available. It was about a gallon-size square jar, much smaller than the crock churn, and easier to use. A paddle on a shaft that fit into gears in a small metal frame screwed onto the top of the glass jar. A small handle protruded from this and was turned by hand until the butter separated. It seemed many things had cranks in one form or another that had to be turned by hand.

My paternal grandparents had a telephone[3] in their home. It was an oak box with a mouthpiece attached to center of the front of it and fastened to the wall about four feet above the floor. The mouthpiece could be tipped up or down to adjust the height of it to accommodate the person using the phone, and the receiver hung on a lever on the left side of the box that disconnected the call when the receiver was hung back on it. On the right side of the box was a small crank that when turned, while holding the receiver to your ear, signaled the operator when you wanted to make a telephone call. It was called a party line. Anyone in that area who had a phone was on the  same line and could listen in, as some people did. Each telephone had a ring signal, such as one long ring and two short rings, etc., so people knew who had a call. When Grandma Koss talked to Aunt Lena or Aunt Grace, they sometimes conversed in German if they thought someone else was listening in on their conversation. A person couldn't make a call when someone else was using the line, just like today.

However, I want to explain how the phone worked. We lifted up the receiver and then turned the crank which signaled the operator who was at a central switchboard in Keokuk. She said, "Number please?" then manually connected your plug into the connector on the wallboard for the number that was requested. She rang the number repeatedly until the call was answered, or she came back on the line with the statement, "They do not answer." We thought that was funny because we knew they did not answer. These ladies were called telephone operators and were employed in this capacity for many years until the telephones were equipped with an automatic dial system and a person could dial the number they wanted. After that, the operators were used for assistance when necessary. Now, when we need assistance, we get a recording and are put on hold listening to music whether we want to or not, and we are often transferred from one department to another until we finally get the one we want. I believe this is called progress. Grandma Jones never had a phone. When they needed a phone, they went to their neighbor's. Grandma never did abuse the privilege; therefore, when she did need to make a call, the neighbors were always willing to let her use theirs. In those days, neighbors were very important, everyone was more friendly hand helpful to each other. We never had a telephone when I was small.

In 1887, Thomas A. Edison invented the phonograph. About 1906, Grandma and Grandpa Koss purchased one of the early designs commercially sold. The records were cylindrical in shape, about two inches in diameter and about six inches in length. Music and comical stories were recorded on them. They had over 100 records. The playing machine was in an oak box with a curved lid. A permanent diamond needle was designed to play the records. Above the apparatus that held and guided the needle on the record was a rubber fitting that a magnifying horn hanging on a tripod stand was attached to. (Somewhat different from the speakers we have today.) On the side of the box was a small crank used to wind up the spring to make the record turn. These phonographs are often shown in museums.

Later, about 1926, when my maternal grandparents moved into the house they owned in Keokuk and Aunt Eunice was ready for high school, they bought a Victrola quite advanced in design. This record player used flat round records called seventy-eights. The player was placed in a tall square cabinet with room to store the records underneath. It was played by winding up the spring by a crank attached to  the side of the cabinet. While I was home we never had a record players. (After I was in nurse's training, my brother, Larry, had a portable electric record player that played the same type of records.) With electronics, compact disks have been designed and used on CD players and in computers with all kinds of information on them.

Mother's parents had an organ that had to be pumped by foot peddles to make it play, and Mother learned to play it when she was young. When we visited my grandparents, sometimes I was allowed to pump the foot peddles and pretend to play the organ. All I knew how to do was to pull out the different stops and play the keyboard, it must have been awful for anyone else to listen to that. Dad bought Mother an upright piano when I was small, and she enjoyed playing church hymns. The first song I learned to sing was "In The Garden." I know all three verses of it and I still like to sing it. While we lived on the farm, Mother taught a Sunday School class. One day, her students came to spend the day. We had a delicious lunch that Mother prepared, and later Mother played the piano, and we all sang church songs.

Some of the farms had deep wells pumped by a windmill. I'm sure all of you have seen windmills, as they are still in operation today on ranches and farms. Neither of my grandparents had a windmill. Their wells were equipped with a pump about waist high that had to be primed to get the water to start to flow and be pumped to fill the water trough for the animals.

On our 80 acre farm Dad installed a small pump inside our kitchen attached to a cupboard called a dry sink. The pump was connected to our cistern, and we were able to prime it  and pump water in the house. We still didn't have any plumbing, so the waste water was collected in a large bucket under the dry sink and when it was full, carried outside and dumped. How wonderful it was not to have to carry water into the house though.

Our house sat back quite far from the main dirt road. To reach it, you had to come up a long dirt lane. As a result there was always a lot of dust blowing and getting into the house in the summer. Screens were on the windows and doors that were kept open for cooling since we had no air conditioning. There was no home air conditioning available for anyone, no modern conveniences for cleaning either. A broom was used to sweep the floors, including the rugs that were too big to shake outdoors. After the dust settled from the sweeping, it was my chore to do the dusting with a soft cloth and furniture polish. The floors were varnished wood with a large carpet in the center of the room. A dust mop was used on the floor area around the rug. The kitchen had linoleum floor covering which Mother mopped.

Mother told this story about my brother, Marty, when he was little. It was the custom between meals to leave the condiments in the center of the dining room table and covered with a pretty embroidered cloth. One day, Marty took the sugar bowl off the table and put little spoons full of sugar all around the edge of the rug in the dining room. Mother really had a difficult time sweeping it up; she probably was never able to get it all out.

Another one of my chores was to feed the chickens that were kept in a fenced area. There was a chicken house with nests for the chickens to nest in at night and to lay eggs in. Every day, I gathered the eggs from the nests and brought them into the house. I had to be very careful not to bang or drop any eggs and break them. One thing I found out, eggs can't be put back together again.

Fences were built with four strands of barbed wire. Once while I was playing, I crawled through the barbed wire fence and caught the side of my knee on one of the barbs on the wire. The barb make a deep gash which Mother cleaned with kerosene (apparently this had an antiseptic effect) and put on a bandage containing a salve made of goose grease. The goose grease had an amazing ability to draw out any infection in a wound. Since the barbed wire was rusty, my wound easily could have become infected, resulting in blood poisoning. With the care Mother gave the wound, it healed up with no trouble. Goose grease was a home remedy obtained from the grease of a goose that had been roasted. When Grandma Koss roasted a goose, she saved some goose grease for us, as we didn't raise geese.

Dad worked hard and steadily to supply us with chopped wood and to grow all our food and grain for the animals besides working for the Du Pont Co. There were certain times of the year when work at the plant was slack and workers were laid off, but Dad kept busy with all the necessary chores on a farm. Mother also worked hard and steady, keeping our clothes laundered, ironed, and mended, and all the food prepared and canned for winter. Mother helped with planting, weeding, and harvesting the garden, and sometimes I helped with the planting and weeding. There were no gymnasiums or exercise programs. Everyone had plenty of exercise from working. They were always thankful for the evening when they were finished and could rest for a little while.

My Dad had fine ash blonde, wavy hair, and my hair was just like his except the waves were missing. One thing I always wished for was to have inherited his waves. Sometimes Mother used a curling iron heated over a lighted lamp to wave her hair, but I never acquired the ability to do that. Her hair was brown and long, and I remember when I was about seven, hair salons began *"bobbing hair"* as it was called. Mother wanted to have her hair cut, but it seemed she had to get permission from Dad. He didn't want her to have it cut, but one day, when she had gone to Keokuk, she decided to have it cut anyway. She thought Dad would like it after he saw it. Well, that didn't happen. Dad was very upset to say the least. Mother had kept the tresses that were cut off, so she fashioned them into a braid and fastened the braids around her head until her hair grew out again. Many years later when almost everyone had bobbed hair, this wasn't a problem anymore with Dad, and Mother wore her hair short with permanents the rest of her life.

Mother had a Singer sewing machine[4] she sewed all of her and my clothes with except for our coats. She made us pretty print dresses, and whenever she made one for herself, and she made one for Dad's widowed sister, Aunt Lena. Whenever she made a dress for me, she made one for my cousin, Mae, who was two-and-a-half years younger than I. Mae was the youngest of Aunt Lena's four children.

Mother made my summer under wear and her own out of white muslin. (She didn't use flour sacks. She made dish towels from them.) The sewing machine was operated by a treadle near the floor that Mother rocked back and forth with her feet. This turned the belt attached to the wheel of the sewing machine making the machine stitch the material as it was guided over the foot feed under the needle of the machine. When she first began using the machine, Mother ran the needle completely through her fingernail and finger. She was careful not to do that again and always cautioned me to be careful when I sewed. Mother was a great believer in the Singer machine and wanted no other kind. This rubbed off on me, and I have always felt the same way. Now there are several very good and dependable sewing machines on the market.

Kerosene (oil) lamps provided our lighting. The lamps usually had a glass base filled with kerosene. A wick about an inch wide and a quarter-of-an-inch thick woven of white cotton string fit into an attachment screwed onto the lamp base. The wick soaked up the oil and was lit by a match. A screw attachment on the side of the fixture controlled the right amount of light by turning the wick up for brighter light and down for dim. If it was turned up too high, the lamp smoked and blackened the glass chimney that fit into a holder to shield the flame.  Every few days, lamp chimneys had to be washed, the wicks trimmed (charred wicks caused the lamp to smoke), and the bases refilled with kerosene.

Another development was the improvement of the lamps. We got an Aladdin lamp for the living room that used a very fragile filament called a mantel, instead of a wick, and was fueled by gasoline. The fuel for the lamp was put into a container that had a small pump on the side and used to pressurize the gas to make the lamp work properly. The lamp provided a much brighter white light than the other lamps, making it easier to read by. A large white glass shade fit over the lamp chimney and was held in place by a wire bracket.

Kerosene lanterns were used outside for chores. These had a tank at the bottom for the kerosene, a glass chimney protected by a wire frame, and a metal frame on top with a bail. The lantern was carried by the bail and hung up by it when you reached your destination. These are still in use today.

We had flashlights with batteries similar to the ones used today. These were used mostly when walking at night, like going down the path to the little square outhouse. When we used the flashlight there, we were careful to put it on the floor. We didn't want the flashlight to drop down into the pit, as it would be very difficult to retrieve.

The Rural Electrification Administration agency, authorized by the Rural Electrification Act of 1936, helped make electricity and telephone services available to people in rural areas. This greatly increased their quality of living and made it comparable to that in urban areas.

When I was about seven years old, there was an airplane[5] show given in a farmer's hay field somewhere in the vicinity of where we lived. Everyone was excited about this, and Dad took our family to watch the show. This was the first time I ever saw an airplane. It had two wings and two seats. The pilot performed many

stunts, like flying low to the ground, then accelerating and going back up in the air, loop the loop, and rolling the plane over in the air. It was scary and thrilling to watch. Rides were offered, and Dad went for a ride in the airplane. The pilot didn't do stunts with passengers in the plane. Although I felt awe and wonder and was excited to see such a demonstration, I certainly didn't realize the importance of this event. I was witnessing history being made.

  Keokuk had a farm team, I think it was called, for one of the major league baseball teams. Because Dad loved baseball, we all went to see a game once in a while. Once, we went to see a fun game with the ball players riding mules. Maybe you know how balky a mule can be; he just wouldn't go where the player wanted him to go. The phrase *"Stubborn as a Mule"* was an adequate expression. Of course this wasn't one of the league games, but it was really funny and entertaining to watch.

  One summer, when I was about seven or eight, Grandpa Koss's nephew, August Koss, brought his family from Detroit, Michigan, to visit Grandpa and Grandma. There were five children in the family and they came in a black seven- passenger automobile. (I think all automobiles were black then.) The car consisted of a front seat, a back seat, and two seats that unfolded in-between the front and back seat. And I seem to remember it was a sedan style with roll up windows. We had never seen an automobile like that. My dad's cousin was in the real estate business in Detroit. They were very nice people, and Mother and Dad invited all of them for dinner. (On the farm, dinner was always at noon). The following Christmas, August sent each family a decorated metal box about five inches square containing a big grapefruit packed with Christmas candy around it. I'd never seen a grapefruit before. Mother split it in two pieces and put sugar on it. It was a little too sour for my taste then. Now, I like grapefruit with no sugar, and when I eat one, I sometimes think of that first grapefruit.

About five years later, August and his family came again for Grandma and Grandpa's Golden Wedding Anniversary celebration. Grandma's daughters, granddaughters, and my mother prepared and served the dinner. The dining table was set many times to accommodate the large crowd. Friends, neighbors, and many relatives from distant cities, whom I had never met before, attended the celebration. One of the sons from the family in Detroit was about my age, and we were pen pals for a few years. It was quite an honor to celebrate a Golden Wedding. Not many couples reached that milestone in their life in those years. Usually one of the couple had some major health problem and died before that goal was reached.

Frequently a Watkin's man called on all the farm people to sell spices, extracts, facial soap, and many other things. One I especially remember was a powdered mix. When water was added to it, it became a delicious orange drink. Sometimes Mother bought this for us, so it was a special day when he came.

While we were living on the Heffner Place, we were friendly with our neighbors by the name of Ruby and Lloyd Knowles and their three children. We were neighbors for about two years, then they moved to a farm near Croydon, Iowa. We were invited to visit them, and that summer we drove to their home about a 100 mile trip. It seemed such a long, tiring, and dusty trip. Marty and I counted telephone poles to help pass the time (the trip took about four hours since we traveled about 25 to 30 miles an hour). We were there overnight, and it rained during that time, making the roads very muddy and slippery all the way home (that wasn't very much fun). After several years, they moved to Plymouth, Illinois. Occasionally through the years we visited each other as my parents remained friends with them.

In the second or third grade, some of the pupils had "strep" throat, although it wasn't called that then. They coughed a lot, and almost everyone seemed to contract it, including me. It left me with severely infected tonsils and a bad cough. Mother and Dad took me to a doctor in Fort Madison, Iowa. Apparently, he was supposed to be able to cure my infected tonsils and cough with medication. That didn't work, however, and the next step was to have my tonsils removed by a Keokuk doctor at the local hospital. I really didn't know just what that entailed, but I found out. After the operation, I was promised ice cream, my most favorite food. But my throat hurt too much for me to eat it, and I remember crying, which made my throat hurt even worse.

We lived on the farm three years when Mother became very ill with severe pain in her right abdominal area. We didn't have a telephone so Dad went to a neighboring farm to call a doctor. I can't remember if the doctor came out or if my father took Mother to the hospital that night. Anyway she had to have surgery for an inflamed, but not yet ruptured, appendix. Her right ovary was also involved and it was removed too. Back then, before the development of antibiotic medicines, a ruptured appendix was usually fatal, and we were all thankful it hadn't ruptured. After Mother came home, she didn't seem to recover. She lost a lot of weight and had a nervous breakdown. I remember little of all this, but sometime in January, the doctor arranged for Mother to go to a special hospital for several weeks to be treated for her nerves. Arrangements were made my brother to stay with Grandpa and Grandma Koss, and I would stay with Dad's sister, Aunt Grace, and her family who also lived on a farm. That put me in a different school district, and I had to transfer to the school there to continue my fifth year.

Aunt Grace cooked differently than my mother. Every morning, we'd have some kind of gruel with milk and sugar. For supper we'd have something shaped like a half a piece of bread (only it wasn't bread) made from the gruel and fried. We probably didn't have it every day, but it seemed like we did. Later I learned this was cooked corn meal and called fried mush. I never did eat it again. One time a few years ago, my husband and I were having breakfast at the Lodge in Big Bend National Park in southwestern Texas. On the menu, grits made from ground hominy, created by treating corn with lye, were included with all the different breakfasts listed. I ordered one of the breakfasts and told the waiter I didn't want the grits. He answered, "You get them anyway." Well, I left them on the plate because they reminded me too much of the cornmeal mush.

Getting back to living with Aunt Grace, one day my head kept itching. Aunt Grace suspected why and checked my head. Sure enough, I had contracted head lice from someone at school. I had never heard of such a thing, but I didn't have the head lice very long. Aunt Grace washed my head with kerosene and then soap. She combed my hair with a very fine toothed comb which got rid of the lice and knits (webs of lice eggs) the lice had planted in my hair. A special medication is used for lice-infested hair now and lice still appears in the schools occasionally.

The hospital the doctor sent Mother to was a psychiatric hospital located in Illinois, which treated all kinds of emotionally and mentally ill patients. The hospital was very expensive, and I believe, privately owned. Mother said the treatment of the patients was very bad and she felt like she was in a prison. All the patients were strapped in their beds at night. No visitors were allowed, and the patients' letters were censored. Mother became friends with one of the aides that worked there, and she agreed to mail some letters for Mother—one to Dad, one to her mother, and one to Dad's sister, Lena. In the letters, Mother explained the care she was receiving and begged Dad to come and get her and not let the doctors dissuade him. Dad went for her and brought her home. You can be sure when she arrived back home, she changed to another doctor. We felt the doctor who had sent my mother there was compensated by the hospital for sending patients there.

NEW FAMILY MEMBER

Chapter 3

BEFORE MOTHER CAME HOME from the hospital, Dad, with helpers, had moved us from our farm to a five room house in the Du Pont Settlement which consisted of approximately 50 homes and divided into two settlements. There were ten bungalow style houses in our row all built alike but painted different colors. Our house was brown. It was spring. I was 10 years old, in the fifth grade, and transferring again to the school I had attended in the first grade. On my first day back to school, I remember coming home and one of the kids trying to tell me I lived in one of the other brown houses. As a child, I was rather shy, and it was a scary feeling not to be sure of which house you lived in.

The roads of the settlements were made from cinders obtained from the plant, I think. Now instead of having light-colored dust, we had black dust to clean out of our house. The roads were never muddy, more like gravel roads, but rough to walk or play on. If you fell down, you ended up with a nasty scrape. Sometimes it was impossible to remove the black discoloration of the cinders from the wound.

The houses were built along the road in groups of four to 10, and all the homes had picket fences around the back yard. Behind the houses were alleys also made with cinders. Across the alley behind each house was a barn and an area for a garden. Inside the back fence was a woodshed, and of course, the little square building called an outhouse. All the houses had electricity and running cold water. A water tower was in one settlement and provided water for the entire area. The only plumbing was a sink with a cold water faucet and plumbing connected to a yard drain that ran through the outside toilets and back to a ravine beyond the garden area—at least keeping the toilets flushed out so they didn't smell quite so rank. The spiders and flies were not eliminated though. There was a water faucet by the outside drain, making water available for outdoor use.

Four houses in the settlements had indoor plumbing and a furnace in the basement for central heating. The plant superintendent and plant bosses lived in these homes with their families.

The electrical wiring in the workers' homes consisted of an electrical cord hanging from the center of the ceiling of each room with a light bulb[6]. There were no wall switches to turn on the lights. The switch was on the fixture that held the light bulb which was difficult to find in the dark and had a tendency to swing away as one tried to turn the light on. The fixture that holds a lamp bulb today is made the same but is usually built into lamps now. A special attachment to the fixture hanging from the ceiling was needed to plug in an extension cord used for appliances as there were no wall sockets. Very few electrical appliances were available. The first appliance Mother bought was an electric iron! What an improvement from having to heat irons on the stove! Having electric lights were wonderful.

We purchased an electric toaster which was tricky to use. While using the toaster, the bread had to be watched, turned to brown the other side, and then removed when it was toasted to one's liking. If we didn't keep a close eye on the bread, it ended up burnt. (No automatic pop-up. When the automatic toasters became available, cartoons in the movies made fun of them by having the bread fly way up in the air when it popped up.) Before toasters, we put our bread on a long-handled fork, then we held the bread over the hot coals in the stove box to toast it. That is the way people toast bread when they camp out.

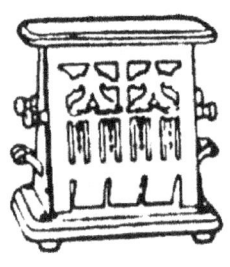

After all the years of washing the clothes on the washboard or with a hand operated washing machine, now with electricity available, my folks bought an electric washing machine. This was a large copper container shaped something like a boiler with ridges in the walls and a hinged lid. It rocked back and forth on a frame operated by a motor under it, swishing the clothes back and forth to get them clean. I don't remember it having a wringer on it, but it probably did. The clothes still had to be rinsed and hung out on the line.

Telephones became more available, but we still didn't have one. I was 10 years old and had never made a telephone call. A small store in a nearby little town delivered groceries to our area. One day Mother sent me next door to use the neighbor's phone to order some groceries. Our neighbor had to tell me how to do it. It must have been a moving experience for me to still remember it.

Keokuk had a movie theater which showed silent movies[7]. When I was about eight years old, Great-Aunt Em Ketterer took me to see one. Aunt Em invited me to stay overnight occasionally and took me to different events she thought I would like. Many times she took me to see a parade or go to the street fair. Keokuk had a street fair every year, featuring free acrobatic feats. One of the acts featured was someone walking on a high wire stretched across a street from one three-story building to another. That was scary to watch as there was no safety net under it. Many special acts were scheduled every year. Side shows were featured, but we never went into any of them. Today, I think how grateful I am for Great-Aunt Em, who took enough interest in me, when I was small, to do all those things for me.

Keokuk was a famous city because of the dam built in 1913 across the Mississippi River. The building of the dam was quite an engineering feat and furnished electricity to a very large area. The power plant is still in operation today and is an attraction many people from all over the country come to see. The dam facility had guided tours, and one summer, when Mother's brother, Uncle Charlie, and his wife, Aunt Inez, came from Davenport,

Iowa to visit us, we all took the tour through the dam. I was in my early teens and found it very interesting. It was

the first time I had ever gone through any kind of a working facility.

Dad's cousin, Marie Ketterer (Great-Aunt Em's daughter), had a touring car, and in the summer of 1927, drove her mother, my mother, and me to Canton, Illinois, to visit my grandmother Jones' sister, my great-aunt Kate. It was a distance of 100 miles, all dirt roads, and it took us four to six hours to make the trip. We stayed a couple of days, and one evening, we drove into Peoria to see a vaudeville show. Peoria was famous for its vaudeville and had a special theater, named the Palace, for the shows. That was a special treat, and we had nothing like it in Keokuk.

In the fall of 1927, Mother still wasn't feeling well, and we went into town to stay with Aunt Lena again. Marty stayed with Grandma and Grandpa Koss on the farm, since Aunt Lena already had a house full, and attended the country school in that area. I don't remember what I did for school that fall, but Dad must have taken me to my school everyday on his way to work at Du Ponts.

In November near Thanksgiving, Mother had a baby boy named Lawrence LeRoy. This was a surprise to me. I was almost 11 and no one had shared that news with me. A lot of people were surprised as Mother hadn't gained much weight. Unlike my older brother and I, born at home, Larry was born in a Keokuk hospital which proved to be a blessing. The babies' temperatures were always taken rectally with a thermometer. The nurse taking care of the new babies, my cousin Bea Franks, discovered Lawrence had a congenital deformity. He did not have a rectal opening—a rare occurrence. Earlier that year, Mother's doctor had been to a seminar about blue babies, a congenital heart malfunction. At the seminar during a break, Dr. Rankin met a colleague in the hall who stopped to chat with him. In the course of conversation, this doctor told Dr. Rankin the experience he had with a congenital deformity and how he had corrected it. This was the very same deformity my brother, Larry, had. Dr. Rankin recalled his conversation and marveled at the coincidence of discussing the same type of deformity and learning how the doctor had made an opening. If this couldn't be done, the baby's condition would become toxic, and he would not survive. Mother's doctor took a metal probe and found an area in the perennial muscle where he could insert the probe to make an opening. He then inserted a glass tube to keep the hole open while it healed. The doctor thought this was temporary and further surgery for a colostomy would be necessary. He didn't think Larry would have any rectal control. When Larry was about nine months old, my parents took him to Iowa City Research Hospital. After the examination, the attending doctors told my parents the opening was fine, working properly, and Larry would not need any further surgery. My parents felt it was really a miracle a general practitioner doctor was able to perform such a successful operation. Dr. Rankin was very proud and wrote this event up in the medical journal. My brother, Larry, told me whenever he has had a physical over the years, he is always questioned about this and how amazed the doctors are when Larry relates the facts to them. (Larry gave me permission to write about this in my book.)

After the baby was born, we went back home to the Du Pont Settlement where we lived. Larry was a small baby, about five pounds at birth, and he had a digestive problem. Mother made a special formula ordered by the doctor which helped Larry retain his food. He gained weight nicely, was a very active and inquisitive child, and received a lot of love and attention from all of us. Our doctor always credited Mother with Larry's survival because of the special care she gave him his first few months of his life.

Mother continued to have trouble with her nerves and unable to sleep. In the spring, the doctor recommended Mother to go to Iowa City Hospital in the Psychiatric Division for treatment. He assured Mother the treatment would be entirely different than at the other hospital, and it was. Mother was in the Iowa City Hospital for about eight weeks and returned home much improved. During this time Dad, baby Larry, and I stayed again with Aunt Lena, and she took care of Larry. Marty stayed with Grandma and Grandpa Koss and helped them on their farm. This was during the summer and didn't affect our schooling. Dad and Aunt Lena took Larry to the Iowa City Hospital for his examination during the time Mother was there. Since Marty helped our paternal grandparents all summer, he continued to stay there for his seventh grade of school.

One of the times we visited Mother at the hospital, we went to a large beautiful park in Iowa City. Mother went with us as it was a nice outing for her. At the park, we saw several ostriches. Seeing these birds strutting around and burying their heads in the sand was an educational experience. I had only seen pictures of them, and it was certainly different seeing them in real life. (Keokuk did not have a zoo.)

Aunt Lena's son, Bud, had a job at the power plant and lived with Aunt Lena and the family. He purchased a player piano, and everyone enjoyed it. He had many rolls of popular songs, and my cousin, Mae, and I spent many hours playing and singing along with them. The rolls had the words of the songs printed on the side of the sheet, corresponding with the notes as the piano played.

Bud also bought a new car, a Chevrolet, that had an electric starter. Bud was always generous and wanted to share whatever he had. One day he wanted my mother to drive his car so she wouldn't have to crank ours. She appreciated the offer but declined.

Around the corner from Aunt Lena's was a small confectionery store we went to when someone would give us a nickel to spend for penny candy. It was a treat to be able to shop for candy as that type of activity was unavailable to us in the country. When Mother was released from the hospital, we returned to our own home. We were fortunate to be a member of a family that took care of each other when there was a need for help.

The next spring, after Larry was born, we moved into the next group of houses in the settlement. The house was painted yellow and was larger with six rooms, three up and three down, and a regular stairway to the cellar. The other houses with one story had a trap door, about the size of a standard door, in the floor of the kitchen that you raised to get to the cellar. It was dangerous when opened, since you could fall into it. We were always careful when it was open and glad we didn't have that kind of a cellar door after Larry began to walk.

We still heated our home in winter with a heating stove in the front room and the cookstove in the kitchen, and the upstairs was heated from a register in the floor above the heater. It was never real warm, but never real cold either, until morning when the entire house was cold.

After we moved here, my parents bought a new kind of an electric washing machine made by the Maytag Company with an agitator for washing the clothes and a wringer. The wringer swiveled over the rinse tubs, and the clothes were run through it from the two tubs of rinse water still necessary to rinse the soap out of the clothes. It certainly made a big difference in the laundry procedure.

Our home had a picket fence around the back yard and made an ideal place for Larry to play. However, Larry didn't like being fenced in, and no matter how Dad rigged up an apparatus to lock the gate without putting a padlock on it, Larry always figured out how to get it open. Larry also checked the fence, and if he found any open space under it, no matter how small it was, he seemed to manage to crawl under the fence. We were never able to leave him in the back yard without supervision.

The year after Larry was born, Mother became afflicted with rheumatoid arthritis. It was a chronic, progressive, and very painful crippling disease from which she suffered the rest of her life. I always felt so sorry that she was in so much pain, but she endured by taking aspirin. She certainly had a lot of stamina, never letting the affliction overtake her, and pushing herself to accomplish what she set her mind to do. She was not a person to be idle or non-productive.

It was 1928, the beginning of the *"Great Depression."* The people living in the big cities had no way of providing their own food. When they were unable to find work, they had no money to buy food from the market. No government relief or aid was available to help them. Soup kitchens were set up by the Salvation Army and churches to feed people that were unemployed

Dad's Aunt Em was a widow, but she took in her daughter, Madeline, and her family consisting of her husband, a little girl, and baby boy born about the same time Larry was born. They had been living in Davenport, Iowa, and Madeline's husband, Alvin, was laid off. As it was the beginning of the Great Depression, many people were out of work, and employment was unavailable. With no money coming in to provide for their needs, many needed help. Our families always helped and looked after each other.

Alvin was quite a creative person and was interested in the new thing called a radio[8]. He spent his free time studying it, and he built a crystal set with earphones attached to it. By putting the earphones on, you could hear music. It was my first introduction to radio (I was about 11 years old).  A couple of years later, friends who lived in Keokuk invited us for a visit to see their radio which was operated by electricity. Due to all the electric wires in the area, the reception had so much static, we had trouble understanding any program. Dad wasn't too enthused about it, but like everything else, it was soon improved. In 1929, my folks bought an Arvin table radio. Quite a collector's item now. My brother, Marty, had it last and took it with him when he went to Hibbing,

Minnesota, to college, but I don't know if he still has it or not. The little table radio was replaced by a cabinet model. Dad enjoyed the radio so much. He especially liked to listen to the baseball games and the news. Numerous comedy programs were on the radio and everyone enjoyed them. *Amos and Andy*, *Fibber McGee and Mollie*, *Little Orphan Annie,* and *The Lone Ranger* were a few of the famous ones. Because crystal sets were inexpensive and easy to build, radio expanded rapidly in the following years. In the 1920s, radio was established as a new mass medium, making it a viable industry and a national forum for news and popular culture.

  In 1929, Aunt Lena remarried and moved to a farm. They had a radio run by batteries which had three dials on the front to tune in a station. It was difficult to get the station tuned in for good reception, but they seemed to make it work. Mae lived on the farm with her mother and step-dad and attended a country school in that area. Aunt Lena's other children continued to live in Keokuk as they were all grown and working.

  When I was older, I accompanied Mother to shop for material for dresses, usually cotton prints. At Penny's Department Store, there were three prices of materials, one group for 10 cents a yard, one for 19 cents a yard, and one for 29 cents a yard. Of course, the prettiest and nicest was 29 cents, but we usually picked some for 19. Once in a while, if I especially like one that was 29 cents, Mother would get it for me. (Mothers are like that.)

  At the age of 13, I made my first dress on the treadle sewing machine. Mother took me shopping for material and a dress pattern, and one day left me home alone to work on my project. By studying the pattern's directions and following the illustrations, I made my first dress. As I continued to sew my own dresses, I decided I didn't want them to look homemade, and I became very particular about the finishing of the garments by carefully following the instructions furnished with the patterns. During these years, a new sewing notion called a zipper was patented and became available in many sizes and colors which enabled you to make plackets in clothing simpler and much neater. Before the zipper became available, snaps or button and buttonholes were used. Now it is hard to imagine life without zippers.

Years later, when I taught my daughters to sew, I told them their dresses could look like they came from a bargain basement, or they could be particular and their dresses could look like they came from the fourth floor of our elegant department store. They both became expert seamstresses and enjoyed making their own clothes through the years. (Their clothes never looked like they came from a bargain basement.)

After I was married, I showed Grandma Koss a pretty dress I had made and she said to my mother, "Hazel, I think she sews even better than you do." I felt quite complimented since praise was never given freely and everyone thought Mother was such a good seamstress.

My grandmother's sister, Aunt Kate, who lived in Canton, was a professional seamstress and sewed for most of the wealthier women in Canton. When I was small, sometimes Aunt Kate would make me a special dress that I wore only to Sunday school and church. One I especially remember was one made from coral satin back crepe with the crepe side out and trimmed with ribbon to match. I thought it was the prettiest dress I had ever seen.

One pretty dress Mother made for me from pink voile I was permitted to wear to school. Ballpoint pens were not invented yet, and we used a pen that had to be dipped into a bottle of ink. I got a big blob of ink on the front of the skirt which was impossible to remove. Finally, someone told Mother to soak the spot in buttermilk and she did. The ink still didn't come out, but the pink coloring of the material around the ink was removed, leaving a big white spot with an ink spot in the middle. That really looked awful, and I felt sorry the dress was ruined and had to be thrown in the rag bag.

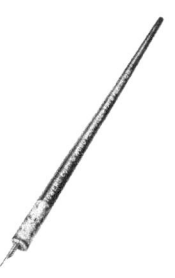

All worn-out clothing and linens were discarded into a rag bag and saved to use for cleaning, then laundered, and used over again. There were no paper towels or disposable materials available for cleaning. And no facial tissues or sanitary products were manufactured until many years later. It is difficult to imagine having to live without those necessary articles.

It was listed in the census Mother's grandmother was a seamstress that sewed for other people. When Grandma Jones was 11, her father was killed by a train accident. Following is the article reported by the local newspaper about it:

THE DAILY GATE CITY, Keokuk, Iowa
September 9, 1883, Wednesday

DEATH BY ACCIDENT.
A Locomotive Runs Over Robert Pipkin—One Leg Crushed and The OtherInjuries Causing

Death in a Few Hours—He Begs to be Killed. The ponderous wheels of a C. B. & Q. passenger engine bore Robert Pipkin down to death yesterday morning. The accident so far as the railroad company was concerned appears to have been unavoidable. The south bound train was a little late in arriving, but a new engineer had command of the throttle and not being familiar with the yard, he brought the train to the depot at a slower rate of speed than usual. Just as the train approached the east end of the platform, Mr. Pipkin attempted to cross the track from the city side of it. The engine was but a few feet fromhim when he started. Several persons called to warn him, but it was toolate. He seemed disconcerted by the danger, turned partially around on his crutches on the platform side of the track, and then the pilot of the engine struck him. He was knocked down and rolled along the track 27 feet before the wheels passed over his limb. The train was stopped quickly, and it was found that one of the driving wheels held him fast. The train then backed, and tender hands pulled the injured man from beneath the engine. He was taken into the depot and remained there until death which occurred at 12:20. A physician at the depot whose name we did not learn fixed a bandage to stop the flow of blood. Dr. J. C. Huges was sent for, but as Mr. Pipkin never rallied, all that could be done was to administer stimulants. Mr. Pipkin was conscious and begged several men by name to cut his throat or take off the bandage from his limb and let him bleed to death. He did not want to live. His family arrived before he died but did not see him, it being thought for the best. The manner in which his right leg was mutilated and crushed was fearful. The limb was severed below the knee and the flesh torn off on the inner side above nearly to the body. His right arm was broken and there were cuts and bruises on the head and face. Mr. Pipkin was blind in the right eye and the left leg had been of no service to him for years. He had served the county in delivering wood to the poor for years and was known by most everyone in the city. It was a difficult matter for him to make a living, and there was talk yesteday that while in despondent moods, he had threatened suicide, but this not confirmed. But few believe that he voluntarily walked in front of the engine to meet death. A coroner's inquest was held. The deplorable accident shows the necessity of a flagman at the foot of Johnson street and at the bridge.

My family had a piece of furniture in the kitchen called an icebox. That is the reason, through the years, I sometimes called our refrigerator an icebox. I was usually corrected by one of my children, as they didn't understand why I referred to the refrigerator as an icebox. The icebox was an insulated oak chest with three doors in the front. Behind the largest door and the smallest door were shelves for food storage. The other door covered the area that held up to a 100 pound block of ice. A small drain hose at the bottom drained the melted ice water into a basin under the bottom of the chest hidden by a long door to conceal the pan. It was necessary to empty the basin, and if forgotten, the result was a big puddle of water on the kitchen floor. You might be rudely reminded if you went to the kitchen for a snack at night, and stepped your barefoot into a puddle of ice water! Every few days, an ice man with a horsedrawn wagon delivered ice to our home. It was a special treat when the ice man give us some ice chips from the wagon. A small truck delivered the ice when cars became more available.

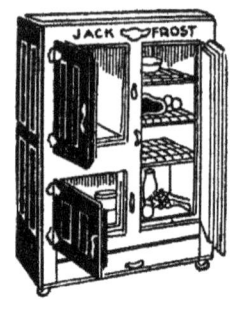

The spring after Larry was born, my Dad bought a one year old 1927 Model-T Ford Sedan. It was very hard to start and still had to be cranked by hand. That year, Mother, Dad, and Larry took Grandma Koss and Aunt Lena to see Dad's sister, Aunt Annie and her family, who lived in southeastern Nebraska. Automobiles didn't have trunks, a bracket was on the back to fasten an extra tire onto. Luggage for a trip was placed on the running board and held on by a gate-like bracket attached to the running board. Martin and I didn't get to go because there wasn't room for all of us. When they returned, Mother brought me the most beautiful coat from Omaha. To me, it was a treasure, and I enjoyed it very much. It was my first new coat. All my other coats were hand-me-downs from one of my cousins. It was the most beautiful color, an off-red of lightweight wool material, and it had a beautiful white fur collar. I was almost grown by then and was able to wear it several years. I didn't "hand it down" to my cousin, Mae. By that time, she didn't wear "hand-me-downs" anymore. I was happy I could keep it, and I made Cheryl a beautiful spring coat from it. I didn't put the fur collar on her coat but bought some Irish Lace as an overlay on the collar. When Pam grew big enough she wore it, so both my girls were able to enjoy it, too.

Two years later, Dad and Mother purchased a new 1930 Model-A Ford Sedan (Marty said they paid $495.00 for it), and they planned a trip to take Grandma to see Aunt Annie again. This time, Marty and I were included, and of course Larry went with us, too. It was about a 400-mile trip over the dirt roads of Iowa and quite hilly. We stopped in Omaha first to visit Grandma's sister, Aunt Meal, and her family. It took us 24 hours to reach Omaha from Keokuk with Dad driving all night. There was no place to stop, as motels were unheard of then and hotels too expensive for us. After a couple of days, we went on to visit Aunt Annie and her family. They lived in a very small town, Henderson, Nebraska, which was 100 miles west of Omaha. Aunt Annie's husband, Uncle George, owned the bank there. It

was during the Fourth of July holiday, and the oldest of my three boy cousins, Junior, enjoyed scaring me with firecrackers. In later years when we traveled west, we often stopped to visit my cousins, Paul and Don, and their families. This was always something I looked forward to as we had such an enjoyable time. Junior died in 1965 at the age of 47.

My dad loved to go fishing for catfish in the Des Moines River near his folk's farm. We went with him a few times with another family. Fishing was better in the evening, and the men used a row boat and strung fishing lines containing many hooks out into the river. The lines were called trout lines, but it had nothing to do with trout fishing. Every hour or so, depending on how good the fish were biting, the men rowed their boat out to check the lines and take the catfish off the hooks. Then they put more bait on the hooks with the expectations of catching more catfish. Sometimes the bait tempted the turtles, and they got hooked. Dad didn't care for turtle so he just chopped their heads off to get them off of the line and let the turtles drop back into the river. The men built a camp fire for warmth and to cook our supper and our breakfast, if the fishing was good, and we stayed until morning. Being there at night, we could hear the crickets singing their song and the frogs croaking theirs. It was truly a fun night sitting around the fire and hearing all the tales being told. The only bad thing about our fishing trips was the mosquitoes. They caused big welts and a lot of itching. Most of the time, Dad usually went with a group of other men. The men cleaned the fish at the river, and the fish were ready to be cooked when they came home.

Florence Wright, who was in the same grade as I, became my good friend, and we are still friends to this day even though we went different directions after high school. She moved to Phoenix, Arizona, many years ago, but we corresponded all through the years. In my travels, I have been to Phoenix a few times and visited her. We enjoyed spending time together reminiscing and catching up on activities of our families. A couple of summers ago, Florence, with some of her family, visited us. That was a real joy.

My friend, Florence, played the piano and we had fun singing with her as she played. She taught me the scale and to play a little, but we didn't have our piano anymore, since my parents sold it when me moved to the Du Pont Settlement. We spent many hours playing *"I Spy"* and a card game named *Flinch*. Her mother was so good to us, and we had lots of good times together. In the summer, we wore all the grass off of their back yard playing croquet. Florence had an older brother, Glenn, and two younger sisters, Vera and Leona. Often we all played together as Marty and Glenn were friends, too. We hiked, ice skated on the lake in winter, and played in the designated swimming area in the lake in the summer. I learned to swim a little but not well. The boys always liked to dunk the girls, and that wasn't very pleasant. A large man-made lake lay between the two settlements with an overflow dam on the end of the lake. Florence and I rode our brothers' bikes when they would let us borrow them, as we didn't have bikes of our own. It was difficult for me to learn to ride a boy's bike, but my cousin, Mae, had a girl's bike, and she let me learn on it.

One day, a group of about 12 girl friends and I hiked over to another friend's near Grandma Koss's, which was about five miles in the country from where we lived. We had blanket rolls and slept out in the woods near their house. In the night, a fierce storm blew in and rained deluges, overflowing the creek at the bottom of the hill near their farm. We scurried into their house and camped out on their floor. The next morning, some of our parents came and took us back home. We were about 14 years old.

Florence's brother got a pair of skis one year for Christmas. One afternoon, we all went to a small hill near the settlement, and he let us take turns skiing down the hill. It might seem weird for me to remember that, but it was quite an experience for someone that had never heard of or seen a ski before.

We walked to school in all kinds of weather (no school buses). The snow drifted high on the sides of the road (at least it seemed high to me, I realize now, because I was small). Sometimes the snow developed a crust on it from thawing and freezing. We liked to see how long we could walk on top of the snow drifts before we broke through the snow. Some days it was so cold the snow crunched as we walked, and our breath made frost on the scarves we had wrapped around our faces.

After completing eighth grade and graduating, all of the rural school students who wanted to go to high school were required to take and pass a written examination given at Donnellson, Iowa. I don't remember if everyone took the examination or if they passed it (but five of us attended and graduated from high school). Since Marty stayed with Grandma and Grandpa Jones in town and attended eight grade at the Junior High in Keokuk, he qualified to attend high school and wasn't required to go to Donnellson to take that test. (He missed that unpleasant experience.)

For a special event on graduation from eighth grade, our school teacher took our class to Fort Madison, Iowa, to tour the Schafer Pen Co where the worldwide famous Schafer fountain pens[9] were manufactured. The expensive ones had gold penpoints and a lifetime guarantee. In grade school, we used a pen holder which held a metal penpoint inserted into a slot on the end the holder. A bottle of ink was used to dip the pinpoint in when we were required to do our lessons in ink, mostly in English and Writing classes. These papers didn't always turn out very neat. After using a pinpoint for a while, the point became bent and had to be replaced. But I think these pens were much better than the quill pens made from feathers that preceded them and were used by our forefathers. Our trip also included a tour of the State Penitentiary in Fort Madison, Iowa, where we had a group picture taken on the steps of one of the buildings. (It was fun to tell people I had my picture taken when I was in the penitentiary).

HIGH SCHOOL

Chapter 4

THAT FALL WE STARTED HIGH SCHOOL, and you may find the following information interesting. A Sinnet Company truck used for delivering or moving furniture was provided for our transportation to high school paid for by the Du Pont Co. This truck had wooden sides and roof and a long bench inside on each side wall of the truck bed for us to sit on. The  back end of the truck was open. We walked about a half mile to the gate house of the plant and waited for the truck. It's surprising, as I think back, to realize no one ever fell out or was hurt by this mode of transportation. (It would not pass OSHA regulations today.) There were a large number of students, but they were fairly well behaved. My brother and I went to high school this way except for my junior year when we were at Grandpa Koss's. My uncle Charlie's desire to go to high school was so great, he walked about four miles to and from school every day. So I'll add, the Sinnet Truck was much better than walking to school. (It was about seven miles.)

When I entered junior high school for my ninth grade, our homeroom teacher asked me what I wanted to do when I graduated from high school. I told her my desire was to be a nurse, and she enrolled me in the college prep course. That was good, because I had no idea what subjects I needed to take. A home room was assigned to us where we met each morning for attendance records and announcements before we went to our classes.

In senior high, my homeroom teacher, Mr. Megchelsen, taught mechanical drawing. Another female student and I decided we wanted to enroll in his class as one of our elective classes. He accepted us, and we were the first female students in that school to take mechanical drawing. It was a course designated for boys. We only took one semester but enjoyed the curriculum, and we both received A's.

Chemistry was another class I enjoyed. Our teacher, Mr. Johnson, made it interesting, and during the school year, he made arrangements for the class to tour the Union Carbide plant which made alloys plus many other things. He took us through the Keokuk Gas Co. where the gas for the city of Keokuk was manufactured from coal and gave us the chemical formula for this process. I have long forgotten what it was. We had very good teachers for our various classes, biology, English, history, and geometry, that I enjoyed. Two years of Latin were required for the College Prep course, and that was not my favorite subject. Now I realize Latin gave me a broader knowledge of the meaning of words I would not have had otherwise.

Some of my other class electives were typing and shorthand, one year of each. If you took the secretarial course, two years were required. I hardly used shorthand,  and what you don't use you lose—an old adage but true. Through the years at various times, typing has been very useful to me in different nursing positions I have had, and especially now, since it enables me to write this story on a computer. I would never be able to accomplish this project any other way. (However, about the only thing similar to the typewriter I had in school are the keys.)

Another elective I enjoyed was chorus and the glee club. I had no prior musical training but that was not required. When I was small and we had our piano, my mother played it, but she never gave me any encouragement to learn to play. As we lived in the country, transportation for lessons probably would have been difficult. A fact I always thought fascinating was one of my teachers, Miss Craig, who taught ancient history and made the subject very interesting, had taught my grandmother Jones in high school.

I was the only one in my senior class from the rural Summitt School who went on to higher schooling after graduating from high school. I thought Florence should have gone to college as she was such a good student, but she didn't. Many of my high school classmates went to college, nurse's training, or apprentice courses, and some went into the armed forces. It was always Mother's dream that her children attend and graduate from high school. I thank her for that. It never occurred to any of us not to go to high school, which enabled me to go to nurse's training and my brothers to college. Marty attended a junior college in Hibbing, Minnesota, to study business. There were not many junior colleges at that time. Larry, after his discharge from the Navy after serving in the Korean war, went to the University of Iowa on the G.I. Bill and graduated in three years with a B.S. with honors in English.

Mother loved school and was very good in all her classes. Her mother had graduated from high school, and Mother's desire was to go to high school, too. She told us after she finished the eighth grade, her teacher made a visit to her home to encourage her parents to let her continue on to high school since she was such a capable student. Her father refused permission for her to go, and said she was needed to help with the work at home for their big family. (Mother always resented this). Mother's youngest sister had just been born. A couple of years later, my dad was courting my mother and proposed marriage to her. She was only sixteen, but Dad was nine years older than Mother and a responsible young man, so they were wed.

One Sunday morning, February 28, 1932, Grandma Jones, at age sixty, died suddenly from a heart attack. She had been overweight and short of breath for many years, but she never went to any doctor. Grandpa and she were planning to go to church, and she got up early that morning. Aunt Eunice was in her senior year of high school and living at home. She and Grandpa thought it strange they didn't hear Grandma moving around. When they came down stairs, they found her sitting in her rocking chair, dead of a heart attack. Being so sudden, this was very traumatic for the entire family.

As my dad's parents aged, every spring, a day was planned by Mother, Dad's two sisters, and the granddaughters to have a house cleaning day for Grandma and Grandpa's home. Big rugs and little rugs were hung outside on the clothesline for the children to beat the dust out of them with a wire frame attached to a handle called a rug beater. It was shaped something like a tennis racquet, only made of wire, and now found in museums. This job usually fell to Mae and me because we were the youngest granddaughters. It was a tiring, hot, dusty job, and we were not too enthused about doing it. We kept inquiring if we had beat them long enough and were happy when they finally said yes. Some people like to hang a rug beater on their family room wall for decor. (I don't want one hanging on my wall!) The adults swept, scrubbed, dusted the walls, polished the furniture, and washed the windows inside and out. By the end of the day, everything was sparkling clean and put back into place. Now it is somewhat difficult to even hire a competent person to clean one's home.

    We had lived in the yellow house three years when Grandpa Koss became ill and unable to take care of the chores on their farm. Families looked after their own, and at a family conference, it was decided my dad and his family (meaning us) should move in with his parents to take care of them and their farm. We moved in after school closed for the year, and Marty did most of the farm chores and the farming that summer. Dad drove back and forth to work at the Du Pont plant. Living on the farm with my grandparents meant we were again living with no electricity. Dad attached a gasoline motor to the washing machine, so it could be used while we were there. Mother wasn't about to go back to scrubbing the clothes on a washboard for a group of seven people. The gasoline engine was very noisy, but it worked fine.

Grandma owned a feisty rooster, and I remember one day the rooster came onto the back patio where Larry was playing and bit him real hard on the calf of his leg. I guess the rooster thought Larry's leg looked like a tempting morsel. But the rooster soon turned into a tempting morsel, when Grandma wrung its neck, cleaned it, and put it in a cookpot with dumplings for our dinner that night.

That fall, a farm auction was held at their farm to sell all the farm equipment and most of the livestock. Some of the livestock was kept for family use, and there were still chores to be done morning and night, Marty attended to most of them.

The summer we lived in the country taking care of my grandparents, I was a junior in high school. Permanent waves given by hair dressers had just been developed. This was accomplished by applying a special solution to the hair and wrapping the hair onto rods. Metal covers attached to a machine were clamped over the rods, and heat was applied to them for a number of minutes, 15 or 20, I think. That summer before school started, Mother supplied me with the money to get my first permanent, and through the years I have continued to have permanents. Since my hair is so fine, the permanents give body to my hair making it appear thicker. I had always shampooed my own hair, and learned how to wrap my hair on curlers to shape my hair into waves. The last thirty years, I have gone to the hairdresser for that task.

That fall, I was a junior, and Marty was a senior. Since we were not living at Du Ponts, we needed to find transportation to school. We were fortunate to obtain a ride with four other high school students living in the rural area. About this time, I started calling Martin Ernest, Marty. He liked that nickname and has gone by it ever since.

Marty enrolled in the shop class where woodworking and other crafts were taught. A project was required, and Marty selected to make a cedar chest for me. He purchased cedar lumber from the shop the school had available for the students' various projects. Marty made the cedar chest very sturdy and finished it beautifully. I have always treasured this piece of furniture.

Larry was four years old, and the country school director asked Mother and Dad if they would consider sending Larry to his school, as there were only five students in that area and six were required to keep the school open. After much discussion, it was decided to start Larry in school, and if it proved to be too much for him, they would keep him home. Sending Larry to school was good for him. He loved it and was able to do all the first grade work. At the end of the year, the teacher advised my parents to let Larry be promoted to second grade, as Larry would probably be very bored if he had to repeat the first grade again. Because he started school at such an early age, Larry was only sixteen when he graduated from high school.

My dad loved to play pinochle. I remember Mother's brother, Uncle Vernie, coming out to the farm to visit. Dad and Uncle Vernie wanted to play pinochle. They needed at least one more to play three-handed pinochle, and they asked me to play. That was my introduction to pinochle. They really only needed me to hold that third hand, but it didn't take me long to learn a few of the fine points of bidding and playing pinochle.

After that, my brother and a neighbor friend sometimes played in the evenings.

Since Grandpa Koss was unable to read English and always interested in the news, every evening Grandma read him the *Daily Gate City* newspaper from front to back. He could always repeat exactly what she read, but Grandma couldn't always repeat it correctly. If she was telling about something she read and didn't repeat it right, Grandpa would always say, "No, no, Mama. Dot is not the vay it vas." Then he would tell it correctly.

We lived with my grandparents for a year, but because of her health, Mother was unable to cope with all the work and the stress of having a house full of company every weekend. One day, she told Dad not to come home from work without a key to a house in the Du Pont Settlement. On his return home, he had a key. Aunt Lena decided she would move in with her parents and take care of them. Her husband stayed on their farm, about two miles away.

We moved back to the Du Pont Settlement in a two story five-room house in the older settlement. The rooms were larger than at the yellow house, and fewer homes were in this area. In this settlement, there had been a boardinghouse for the men employed at the Du Pont plant. At one time, when Dad was single, he worked at Du Ponts and lived at the boardinghouse. The boardinghouse was no longer there, but there were two other company buildings in use. One was a dance hall and the other, a two-story building, called the clubhouse. The clubhouse had pool tables on the main floor and tables upstairs for playing cards. The floors were hardwood oak flooring. When the dance hall was removed, the clubhouse was used for all activities. Square dances and round dancing were held at the clubhouse now. It was a big building and had plenty of room. I didn't dance very well, but I had fun trying. Many parties were held there over the years.

Since we were back to electricity, we were also able to use our toaster and electric iron again. Happy day! By this time I was doing a lot of ironing and it was a real chore to iron with the flat irons. I wonder if my brother, Marty, remembers all the white twill duck pants I ironed for him. They could only be worn once and then rewashed and ironed again.

Electric vacuum sweepers were being manufactured, and my parents bought a Hoover sweeper with attachments. It was a wonderful appliance for cleaning. To really appreciate this appliance, try cleaning without it for a month.

Marty had graduated, and I was a senior back to walking down to the gatehouse to ride the Sinnet truck to high school. We finally had a telephone put in our home. At first, we had a small box telephone on the wall. Later my parents bought a desk and ordered our phone changed to an upright phone. All telephones were owned by the telephone company. Both styles are pictured to the right.

My parents also purchased an electric Singer sewing machine and a special attachment for it that made buttonholes. The buttonhole attachment was a pleasure to use, and my dad was intrigued by this apparatus. He didn't use it himself, but he enjoyed watching it work when we used it. Buttonholes were always difficult to make neat by hand. Only my grandma Jones was proficient at doing that.

Since we had moved back to the Du Pont Settlement, Larry attended the same two-room school where Marty and I had started school. Mother was appointed director of the school and remained director for many years. One of the important tasks was to hire the school teachers. One year a teacher, Esther Buck, from Denmark, Iowa, about forty miles north of the school, was hired. She didn't want to drive that distance every day and needed a place to board near the school. Marty was in a junior college in Hibbing, Minnesota, and I was in Peoria in nurse's training. Only one at home was Larry, so my parents had a room for Esther, and she boarded with them for many years.

After Marty finished his courses at college, he obtained a job in Keokuk and moved back home with Mother and Dad. One day Esther introduced her sister, Leola, to my brother, Marty. About two years later, they married in August of 1942. In December of that year, Marty was drafted into the service of World War II. He was in the service for 39 months, spending 29 of those months in England with the rating of Staff Sergeant. After being discharged from the service, Marty was employed as a manager for the Kroger grocery chain and eventually settled in Burlington, Iowa, where he and Leola raised their family. Marty and Leola celebrated their golden anniversary in 1992. They have three children, Merrill, Lynette, and Lyle. Lyle and Lynette stayed in Burlington, married, and had families. Merrill served in the Vietnam War, was injured, and received the Purple Heart Medal. After he was discharged, Merrill stayed in California, married a girl he had known when she lived in Burlington,

Iowa. Before she and her family moved to California, her father was a minister at the Burlington church Marty's family attended When Merrill was stationed at Camp Pendleton, California, in the service, he wrote to them and was invited to their home.

In the fall of 1933, about a year-and-a-half after Grandma Jones died, Grandpa Jones was severely injured while working at the Electro-Metals, a factory that made pig iron out of scrap metal. A huge metal bucket, attached to an overhead crane, was unloading scrap iron from a railroad car my grandpa was working in. The man controlling the crane gave the signal for the operator to proceed before Grandpa was in the clear. The bucket struck him in the back, pinned him against the scrap, and crushed his pelvis. Due to his injuries, Grandpa's bladder was unable to empty, and a tube had to be inserted through his abdomen for drainage. His injuries were so extensive the doctors were at a loss to help him, and after eight weeks, he died as a result of the accident. If the accident had happened more recently, with the advancement in medicine, I'm sure the doctors would have been able to save him. Grandpa was a very hearty, active person, and no doubt he would have lived many more years had this not occurred.

The following January in 1933, Grandpa Koss passed away. Grandma sold her farm and stayed with us for about six months. That spring, Roosevelt was president, and he closed all the banks for three days. Some of the banks were unable to reopen, including Aunt Annie's husband's bank in Henderson, Nebraska. The family was in dire straits with no money and no food. Dad went to Nebraska and brought the entire family to Keokuk. Aunt Annie and Uncle George stayed with us from June until fall, and Grandma and the three boys,

Junior, Paul, and Donald, moved on the farm with Aunt Lena and her husband. In September, Dad took the family back to their home in Nebraska with the exception of the oldest one, Junior. He was employed by a local farmer and stayed in the area, met, and married a local girl. While Junior was in the service of World War II, he wife became ill and died. After being discharged from service, he returned to his family in Nebraska.

    Grandma Koss continued to live with Aunt Lena until she passed away at the age of 86 in 1944. She spent her time making beautiful embroidered pillowcases for her church bazaars, and as Christmas presents, and sold them to anyone wanting to purchase any. She helped Aunt Lena with stemming and cleaning any vegetables or fruits Aunt Lena was cooking or canning. Grandma was never one to have idle hands. It was important for her to be productive.

    About 1938, due to poor circulation, Grandma developed gangrene in one of the toes on her right foot. This condition resulted in her having her leg amputated above the knee. There was difficulty with the stump of the leg healing, and the doctor ordered a special bed. A motor attached to the bedframe created a rocking motion of the bed which stimulated Grandma's circulation and enabled her leg to heal. She continued to use this bed until her demise. Grandma's hair was very fine and black with very few gray hairs when she died. One time someone asked her if she colored her hair with shoe polish. You can imagine that made her quite indignant. She was very proud of her dark hair.

    After I graduated from high school in 1934, I was only 17 and not old enough to enter nurse's training. The superintendent of Du Pont, Mr. Myers, and his wife needed someone for cleaning, cooking, and on occasions, looking after their little three-year-old girl. They came to my house and asked me if I would work for them. The pay was five dollars a week, with extra pay, 30 cents, when I took care of the little girl, Lizabeth. I didn't work on Sundays and had every afternoon from 1-4 free unless I took care of Lizabeth. I sometimes took care of her in the evenings, too. The laundry was sent out. Sometimes, they gave a dinner party but engaged another person to take care of it, and I helped with the serving and cleaning up.

That fall, Mr. and Mrs. Myers and their daughter went east to visit Mr. Myers' relatives. On their way back they wanted to stop in Chicago to shop for a few days. They made plans for me to meet them in Chicago at the Palmer House Hotel, so I could take care of Lizabeth. I went by train from Keokuk to Burlington, transferring there to the train to Chicago. A new experience for me; my first train ride and by myself. On the train, I needed to use the restroom which was located at the end of the train car over the wheels. The train jerked back and forth so much, I was unable to relieve myself. It was probably due to nerves. When I arrived in Chicago, I took a cab (a short way from the train station) to the Palmer House. Was I ever glad to get to the room, so I could use a toilet that didn't move, as by then I was miserable.

Mr. and Mrs. Myers went shopping while I took care of Lizabeth. She liked to be read to, and there was also a play room in the hotel for children where we spent some time. In the evening, we went to a dining room in the Palmer House for dinner. There were several beautiful crystal chandeliers hanging from the ceiling and a string orchestra that played lovely music while we ate, all very elegant. Mr. and Mrs. Myers ordered an oyster cocktail with their meal and asked me if I wanted the same, and I agreed (I didn't know what it was). When the cocktails were served, a small glass stood in the center of the plate filled with a red sauce, and around the plate were five oyster shells containing uncooked oysters. Well, I hardly ate them cooked, and here they were on my plate, raw. I watched Mrs. Myers, and then I also took an oyster with my little oyster fork, dipped it in the sauce, and swallowed it whole. I didn't attempt to eat another one. They saw I wasn't eating the oysters, and they asked if I'd like to give the rest to them. That was a relief. I still don't eat raw oysters. The sad part is, I can't remember what else I had for dinner.

The next day, we went to Marshall Fields, a department store a-block-and-a- half square and several stories high with elevators and escalators. I had never seen a store like it. Mrs. Myers shopped for dresses for Lizabeth. If I bought anything, I don't remember. We were in Chicago about three days, and we drove back to Keokuk in their new 1934 Buick through Peoria, Illinois. At that time, I never had any idea I would live most of my life in that city.

After I was eighteen, I applied for nurse's training at St. Joseph School of Nursing in Keokuk. I didn't pass the physical because my urinalysis showed there was albumen, which meant, I had a kidney problem. It was scary, as my Mother's sister had "Bright's Disease" as it was called then, which was a severe kidney ailment. She was very sick for two or three years and died at age nineteen. Mother took me to a chiropractor for several spinal adjustments. After that, I was never told I had a kidney problem again.

I continued to work for the Myers until spring when I left to find a different kind of work. That wasn't so easy. Most of the clerks in the stores were older and had been employed for a long time. I asked my dentist, Dr.

Sinott, if he needed anyone. He hired me to collect some past due bills and gave me a list of the names, addresses, and amounts due. I walked all over Keokuk to the different homes. I was somewhat surprised to have fairly good luck collecting, and my pay was one third of what I collected. However, the job didn't last more than a couple of months.

That summer I was 18, and Mother thought I should learn to drive our car, a Model A-Ford which had an electric starter. It did not have an automatic shift like the cars have today. You had to use a clutch to shift gears. This was a little tricky. In order not to make the car jerk when putting it into motion, you had to develop coordination of letting up on the clutch and using the correct speed at the same time. Mother taught me how to drive, and then I was required to pass a written test and a driving test to receive my driver's license.

Marty had been driving for a couple of years, and when we all went some place together, he didn't want me to drive as he wanted to drive. Male chauvinist. Mother insisted that I was going to drive, so I did, but I never drove the car by myself before I left home for nurse's training.

Marty became very active in Boy Scouts, working hard on many projects and earning his Eagle Badge. He remained active in scouts and was an assistant scoutmaster for many years. At that time, as far as I know, there were no Girl Scouts or Brownies in our area.

LEAVING HOME

Chapter 5

YOU PROBABLY HAVE BEEN WONDERING when and how I finally ended up as a nurse. Here's that story. The fall of 1935, my great-aunt Kate, who lived in Canton Illinois, visited us. Mother seemed to be a favorite of hers, and Mother felt the same way about her. Since I was not working, Aunt Kate invited me to visit her for awhile. She knew many people in Canton and soon found me a job clerking in a variety store, where everything was sold but food and furniture.

I was in Canton all fall, and because I was still interested in becoming a nurse, I talked to Aunt Kate about nursing schools in Peoria. She got the addresses for me, and I wrote to the three nursing schools in Peoria for information regarding their curriculum. Proctor Hospital was an endowment hospital Mr. J.C. Proctor, a wealthy Peorian, had helped finance. He had set up a fund for the nurses enrolled in the nursing school at Proctor. After the nurses passed their probationary period, the fund provided them with a small monthly stipend which interested me. No tuition was required since the student nurses in training gave most of the care needed to the patients. However, we were required to purchase our uniforms and books, but our room, food, and laundering of uniforms were provided by the hospital. I sent in my application to the Proctor School of Nursing with my grades from high school. Shortly, I received an appointment for an interview. Since Aunt Kate didn't have an automobile because she didn't drive and was a widow, she arranged with some of her friends to take us to Peoria. I had my interview, was accepted, and was scheduled to begin my training as a mid-year student, starting the first week of February, 1936.

They informed me I could make my own uniforms and where to get the pattern and material for them. The uniforms were made of blue-and-white gingham fabric with short sleeves and white collar and cuffs. A white apron with a full gathered skirt was worn over the uniform. The bib part of the apron was separate and issued by the hospital to the students when they had completed and passed their first three months of studies. A dressmaker, Aunt Kate was well acquainted with the department stores in Peoria and took me to Block & Kuhl's for the material and pattern. I had saved my money from working at the variety store and had enough to purchase the material to make the six uniforms required. Three uniforms were needed every week to wear and three would be in the laundry. The white collar and cuffs were purchased through the hospital.

I worked in Canton until Christmas, then went back home to Keokuk to make my uniforms before starting my training the first of February. My sewing was completed in time, but it was a difficult task to sort and plan the packing of my suitcases. Since Peoria was quite far from Keokuk, I probably would not be able to go back and forth very often, so I had to make sure I took everything I wanted to use. When I graduated from high school, I had received a very nice suitcase that had hangers in the top half for my good dresses, skirts, and blouses. No one wore slacks. I had two other plain suitcases for the rest of my wardrobe.

About 8:00 a.m. on Sunday morning, I left Keokuk by train traveling 40 miles to Burlington, Iowa. There, I changed trains and rode as far as Mommouth, Illinois, again changing trains to Galesburg. At Galesburg, I boarded another train that stopped at every small town between there and Peoria. Later I learned it was an interurban, operated like a street car. Peoria was about 120 miles east of Keokuk, but as you can probably guess, this was an all-day trip going such a roundabout way. (I probably could have traveled by bus and made the trip a lot quicker, but I hadn't checked on that mode of transportation.) I arrived in the Peoria station about 5 p.m., and being February, it had already turned dark. I took a cab to the Proctor Hospital nurses' residence, which was about a mile from the depot.

I reported to the hospital the next morning for a three-year training course. Mother and Dad helped me with the purchase of my first books. When the rest of our books were issued to us for the different classes, the cost of the books and my nurse's cape was deducted from the monthly allowance the endowment provided for the nurses by Mr. Proctor.

Most hospitals with a training school offered a diploma program to high school graduates. The course was three years, and nurses were taught right in the hospital. They worked every shift and on every floor in the hospital with little time free. The classes were held from September until June, but the student nurses were required to work at the hospital through the summer with only two weeks off. None could be married. If a student married, she was immediately terminated. There were no male nurses, but the hospital employed an male orderly to help with various treatments that he had been trained to perform. A few hospitals were connected with a university and offered a four-year program with a Bachelor of Science degree. For this type of school, the tuition was quite high and not affordable to me. Diploma programs are now obsolete because nursing schools have been taken over by universities offering two year courses for an Associate's degree and four year courses for a Bachelor of Science degree.

Proctor was noted for being a good school. Anyone going to that school received good training. A very high percentage of the students passed the state boards to receive their license required by the state. There were no interns at Proctor which meant the nurses were given some of the tasks that would ordinarily be carried out by interns. This gave us more experience and training not available to the nurses in the larger hospitals.

I felt fortunate for choosing such a good school with the guidance of Aunt Kate. She knew something about this school because a cousin of hers, Nellie McGlaughlin, had graduated from there in 1912—quite a number of years before I started or was even born. I remember meeting her when I was small. She came from Canton with Great-Aunt Kate two different times to visit my grandparents. The first time she was working as a school nurse in Peoria, and the other time she had taken a position in Wisconsin working as a nurse on an Indian reservation. She remained in that position until her retirement.

About the second night I was in Peoria, I was awakened from a very sound sleep by a loud siren. It sounded as if it was coming right through our building, but it roared on by. Our nurses' home was located on a busy street which was a thoroughfare for fire engines. Being from a rural area in the Du Pont Settlement, I had never heard any loud noises like that. I had only heard *Whippoorwills*, *frogs*, and *crickets*.

There were three students enrolled in this mid-term class. For the first three months in training, we were probationers. We spent that time in the classroom with a heavy load of studies. With only three of us in the class, we really had to know our lessons. During question time in class, it didn't take long before it was your turn to answer another question. We also had some clinical instructions on making beds, bathing patients, cleaning equipment, and making supplies. Supplies and treatment trays used on the floors and in operating room were made by the students. This consisted of twisting cotton on wooden sticks to form applicators, cutting and folding gauze squares for dressings and sponges, stretching the laundered used gauze, and refolding it. We made up an assortment of treatment trays with certain prescribed equipment. These were sterilized in the autoclave and made ready for use. Rubber products were used as this was before plastic was made, and we had no throwaways. Everything required thorough cleaning. The nurses assigned to the operating room ran the autoclave (steralizer).

After passing the exams for the subjects we had studied, we were promoted to wear the white bib that made up the rest of our uniform and our nurse's cap. We were not *"Probies"* anymore. During our training, the three of us mid-year students were placed in some of the classes of the group of students that had started the fall before we did. We also were placed in some of the classes of the group that had started the fall after we entered, and this is the group we graduated with.

Because Proctor was not equipped with a laboratory necessary for teaching our science subjects, we were sent to Bradley University for chemistry and bacteriology. Our pediatric floor did not meet the state standards because of its size and small number of patients, and our class was sent to St. Francis Hospital for three months as affiliated students. During the term, we resided in their nursing home but went by cab to Proctor to attend our other classes.

When Great-Aunt Em learned I was going to Peoria to enter nurse's training, she gave me the name and address of Dad's cousin, Minnie Getz, (her mother and my grandmother Koss were sisters). After Minnie married Theodore Klepfer, they moved to Peoria and had a family of two girls and three boys. When they were small, Aunt Em went to Peoria for quite a length of time to help Minnie care for her family.

After I finished my probation studies, I called Minnie on the telephone, explaining who I was and what I was doing. She invited me to come to see them when I had free time and gave me directions how to get there by bus. Her daughter, Eleanor, was my age, and her daughter, Ruth was a senior in high school. All of the family made me feel welcome. I felt very fortunate, it was like a second home to me, and I usually spent my free time with them. Ted, Minnie's husband had a trucking company that transported cargo all over the United States. Eleanor and the two older boys, Bob and Bernard, worked with their dad in the business. Ruth and Richard, the younger children, were in high school. Eleanor did all the office work for the company, and the boys drove the trucks. They had quite a fleet of trucks and also employed other drivers.

Eleanor and I did many things together, but my free time was limited. In training, the student nurses had one-half day off during the week, and all of the nurses were on duty for a half-day on Sundays. Sometimes our free half-day would fall on Saturday afternoon,. and our supervisor would schedule our half-day off for Sunday morning. This made a nice weekend since we didn't report for duty until 1:00 p.m. Sunday. I could request an overnight leave, enabling me to spend this time at Klepfers. We were on duty eight hours a day from 7 a.m. to 7 p.m. with three hours off during the day and a half-hour for lunch and dinner. Once in awhile we'd be scheduled to work straight through from 7 a.m. to 3:30 p.m. On these days in the summer, I could go to Klepfers, as we didn't have to report back into the nurses' home until 10 p.m. The training school kept close tabs on all our activities, requiring all students to sign out when they left and to sign in on their return.

One day in the fall of 1936 during my first year in training, Great-Aunt Kate, who lived in Canton, Illinois, was getting ready to come to see me. One of her friends planned to bring her to Peoria. Very suddenly, that morning, she became ill and died of a stroke just before her friend was to pick her up. I'm so glad it didn't happen on the way to Peoria. I missed her very much and was so thankful I had the Klepfers to call my family.

In the summer, we were given two weeks leave from the hospital school of nursing, and I always spent this time at home in Keokuk. One summer when I arrived home for my two weeks leave, Mother and Dad had purchased an electric refrigerator. Production of electrical appliances for the home had increased, and the price had become more affordable for the working people. This was wonderful, not having to buy ice or make sure the drain pan was emptied. The refrigerator was more efficient as it was colder and kept the food better than an icebox. Refrigerators were designed with the cooling unit fastened inside, in the center, of the top of the of the refrigerator and contained three ice cube trays. Ice built up on the unit and required defrosting about every two weeks. This was before automatic defrosting had been developed. To defrost it, boiling water was put in the ice cube trays and placed in the unit to melt the ice. Dad and Mother also purchased an electric range for their cooking and disposed of the big cookstove.

Another improvement was made. Instead of a wood heater in the living room, my parents installed an oil heater. A tank was stationed on the outside of their home for the oil with a pipe connected from the oil tank to the heater. An oil company serviced their tank to insure it didn't run dry, and that ended the necessity for Dad to provide wood for heating and cooking. Later, Dad moved the heater to the cellar and fitted it with heat pipes and registers into the rooms.

From September until May during classes, we had to be in the nurse's residence at 8 p.m. to study. On Friday and Saturday nights, we were allowed to stay out until 10. When we were scheduled on night duty, we worked from 7 p.m. to 7 a.m. every night for a month, then we had two free days. During the night, there was one float nurse on duty, and if the hospital had a quiet night with no emergencies and no baby deliveries, she relieved each one of the nurses stationed on the different floors for a two-hour period. Otherwise, we stayed on duty straight though the night. Being on night duty was difficult for me since I became very sleepy in the wee hours of the morning. I really had to work at staying awake when none of the patients needed care.

Our time in training was quite regimented. Proctor was a 100-bed hospital. Most hospitals at that time had 50 to 250 beds. I completed my training in February 1939, and Proctor Hospital hired me to work doing floor duty. We were included in the graduation exercises held the first of June, 1939.

Many new drugs to fight infections were beginning to be developed, and the doctors were just starting to use some of them toward the end of my training. Being tested were the Sulfa drugs administered for bacterial diseases, such as puerperal fever, scarlet fever, erysipelas, meningitis, pneumonia, and bacteremia. All the sulfa drugs are somewhat toxic. Kidney damage occurred, and blood abnormalities were produced when the drug was used indiscriminately.

The use of sulfa drugs somewhat declined after the discovery of penicillin, which is as effective as the sulfa drugs and far less toxic. Penicillin was first observed in 1928, but 10 years elapsed before penicillin was concentrated and studied by scientists, making it available to doctors to begin to use it in the early '40s. Many antibiotics have been studied and produced since then. Having them available for use during World War II saved many lives in the armed forces. The advancement of medicine, nursing care, Xray therapy, and surgical procedures has been tremendous in the past 60 years. I would have to write another book to give justice to all of it.

STARTING A NEW LIFE

Chapter 6

WHILE IN TRAINING, I met a young man by the name of Harold Lester Potter who lived in Peoria. He was employed in the printing department of the ABC Washing Machine Co. in East Peoria. Harold and another employee were pushing a cart loaded with paper supplies up an incline. The other employee let all the weight of the load go against Harold, causing him to have an inguinal hernia. He was sent to Proctor Hospital to have this repaired. At that time, patients were kept in bed longer after surgery, and he was in the hospital about 10 days, and I was assigned to his care. (Now it is a surgical procedure performed in the outpatient department.)

    After he returned home and given permission by the doctor to drive a car again, he called me and invited me to a dinner and a movie. We continued to date and became engaged. I wanted to make my own wedding dress. Eleanor liked to sew and had her own sewing machine, and she informed me I was welcome to use it when I had time off. I chose white lace and white satin material for a slip to wear under it, and thanks to Eleanor's generosity, I was able to make my dress.

    After I completed my training in February, Harold and I were married on March 19, 1939, in our church in

Keokuk, Iowa. It was an unbelievably warm beautiful day for that time of year. My parents gave a dinner reception in the clubhouse at the Du Pont settlement for all the relatives following our wedding.

This was also my mother and dad's Silver Wedding Anniversary. Afterward, I felt this wasn't really fair to them, since it took away from their special day, but Uncle Charles and Aunt Inez didn't forget them. They gave Mother and Dad a Toastmaster, one of the first automatic toasters on the market, and they enjoyed it for many years.

Harold's family, like mine, was family-oriented, sharing many activities and holidays together. Harold's dad had three married sisters, two in this area and one in Texas. One sister, Aunt Kate, married to Bill Allen, had no children. The other sister, Aunt Lillie, married to Grover Bagley, had two recently married sons about the same age as Harold. The older son, Gordon, was married to Ann, and the second son, Jerry, was married to Kathleen. We attended the same church and had many good times together. All the family members celebrated special occasions. Harold had one younger brother who married just before he went into the service of World War II. Aunt Flora's husband had a shoe store in St. Louis, Missouri, and had an opportunity to open a store in a large department store in Fort Worth, Texas. They moved there, had a family of two daughters and a son, and lived there the rest of their lives.

Ann and Kathleen belonged to a pinochle club with six other young women. One of the group dropped out, and I was invited me to join. This was a fun group, and we were together 14 years. Many of us were pregnant at the same time, so our children were about the same ages. We often had family get-togethers in the park, and the children enjoyed that. We have continued to see each other over the years. I often play golf with Ann and bridge with Ann and Kathleen.

While Harold was employed at ABC, he was transferred to the pay-roll department and soon promoted to be in charge of it with six girls working under him. His job was to keep track and tabulate all the employees' work hours and the amount of the wages due them. Six employees operated Key Punch machines that punched holes in cards to record the information taken from the employees' time cards. By running the cards with the holes punched in them into a machine, the machine retrieved information from the holes in the cards. It tabulated the number of hours worked times the rate of pay, and the total amount due the employees for their weekly wages was determined. It was a responsible job, and Harold proved he was quite capable to perform it.

Harold and I rented and furnished a small house in East Peoria. We bought a gas stove for cooking and also purchased a refrigerator, as these were not furnished with the house. Since Harold worked for the ABC Washing Machine Co., he was able to purchase a washing machine directly from the company for wholesale price. We felt that was a break for us, since our finances were limited. We had phone serviced installed, and the style of phone was improved to a cradle phone. Moving to East Peoria was a good choice, as it was  easier for Harold to get to work. It has been a very nice place to live with good churches and a good school system for our children.

Harold and I thought I should continue working after our marriage. However, the hours I was on duty were split, and I spent so much time on the bus we changed our minds and I left my job. At this time, Harold continued working at ABC. The pay scale was not too great for office employees, but we managed to get by.

Some of the nurses engaged in private duty. For a small yearly fee, you could list your name on a registry at the hospital. As your name came up, the hospital notified you of a patient requesting a private nurse and to report for duty. This was not very steady work, but I decided to try it. When my turn for a case came up, I was notified and worked on a few cases.

The private duty nurse worked *"20 hour duty"*, which required the nurse to stay overnight to take care of her patient with four hours off in the afternoon. A small cot, supplied by the hospital, was put in the patient's room for the nurse at night. This cot was slid under the patient's bed in the daytime. (There were no electric beds like there are today.) The hospital beds were built high, making it easier for the nurse or doctor to care for a patient. For elevation of the back or foot rest, cranks were attached at the foot of the hospital bed, and it was necessary for the nurse to crank (still necessary to use cranks) the bed to the elevation ordered by the doctor or requested by the patient. A footstool was provided for the patient to use with the help of the nurse to get out of bed when the doctor ordered it. A nurse's community dressing room provided by the hospital gave the nurse a place to change into a nightgown and robe for the night hours. Anytime the patient needed or wanted anything, he or she awakened the nurse to take care of it. (I can't imagine anyone working like this now.)

If a patient was very ill and needed constant care, a nurse was employed for 12 hours. Usually there were two nurses on the case like that, but sometimes a patient would rely on floor care in the daytime and have a nurse from 7 P.M. to 7 A.M. A nurse was self-employed and hired by the patient or the family, and one or the other was responsible for the bill to the nurse. I also worked as a relief nurse in the dispensary at ABC Washing Machine Co. By my working part-time, we were able to save this extra money and buy a lot to build a house on.

Before our first child was born, because of the low wage scale at ABC, Harold decided to look for work elsewhere. He applied and was hired by Caterpillar Tractor Co. also in East Peoria. With Harold's previous work experience, Cat wanted to hire him in the office, but Harold felt the wage scale working in a production capacity was much greater than office work. The reason for his decision to work in the plant was to qualify for the apprentice course offered by Cat. After six months, he was eligible to enter their two-year apprentice course. He became a toolmaker and worked for Cat many years.

When we were first married and since I liked to sew, someone gave us a treadle sewing machine. Harold attached a small electric motor, I operated by a foot pedal, to the wheel of the sewing machine. This made the machine easier to use, and I continued to make my own dresses. While expecting our first baby, from my experience in the hospital taking care of children, I remembered how difficult it was to keep the crib sheets straight. I had an idea how to fashion some sheets for the baby crib to correct that problem. I bought sheeting by the yard and by fitting the material on the mattress of the crib, I mitered the corners of the sheets. (These are called fitted sheets now.) That way, the sheets stayed on the mattress instead of getting all wadded up under the baby.

After Jim, our son, was about three months old and the nights were cooler, it was difficult to keep covers on him when he moved and kicked his legs which caused him to be cold in the night. I had another idea. I took one of his crib blankets, folded it with the ends meeting in the middle, stitched a zipper on the edges so it could be zipped on and off Jim, and stitched it across the bottom and the shoulders, leaving openings for his arms and head. This worked so well to keep him warm, I used the same idea for all the children when they were babies. (These are called sleepers now.)

A few years later, you could purchase fitted bed sheets to fit all sizes of beds. Also sleepers, with arms and legs fashioned in them, made of different weight material for different seasons of the year, were manufactured for children. Too bad, I didn't have the knowledge or "the know how" to market my ideas. One new article available was little rompers made of cotton knit with snaps for changing diapers. These were so cute and easily laundered, and I used them for both our boys.

We were able to start building our new home before our first child, James Martin, was born on August 15, 1941. Harold engaged different people to do some of the work, but his family, my family, and Harold did most of the work. It was a nice, but small home with hardwood floors. We moved into it the following February and lived there 16 years. In that time, we had another son, Jerry Melvin, born October 11, 1944, and two daughters, Cheryl Marie, born February 6, 1947, and Pamela Joy, born September 4, 1951.

The following November after Jim was born in 1941, Japan engaged in a sneak attack, bombing Pearl

Harbor, sinking many of our ships stationed there, and killing a very large number of our service men. That incident caused the United States to enter World War II which had started about two years before by Hitler attacking and conquering the smaller countries in Europe near Germany and then bombing England. These years were sad years with so many of our young men killed or seriously injured. In the beginning of the War, Harold, because he was married and a father, was deferred. As the war progressed, Caterpillar had him deferred because of his training as a toolmaker, since his expertise was needed in the manufacturing of war equipment.

For me, the war years also hold memories of shortages of shoes, sugar, gasoline, meat and several other commodities I don't remember. We were issued stamps to entitle us to buy those things; thus, it controlled how much any one family could purchase. This prevented people from hoarding scarce items. Victory gardens were encouraged to supply extra food, and most every one participated in that endeavor. There was no television yet, but the war news was always on the radio. When we attended movies, which was usually our only recreation, newsreels of the war action were shown on the screen. We were always interested and glad of the opportunity to see the action pictures of the war.

A very sad occasion occurred in the war conflict in Europe. During the *Battle of the Bulge* in Bastogne, France, my cousin Robert Klepfer was one of the many soldiers killed in action..

Mother was active in the war effort, especially with Marty being in the service and stationed in England. She joined the American Red Cross and worked for their drives, knitted articles for the service men, and helped in any capacity she could. Mother was quite patriotic and proud of our country.

The European War ended in May 1945, but the war with Japan was still in operation. The Atomic bomb had been developed at the Los Alamos Research Laboratory in New Mexico—at that time a secret city. No one but the people that were employed there and the government agency, the Department of Energy, that controlled it, knew of its existence. An atomic bomb was tested at Alamagordo, New Mexico, on July 16, 1945

Japan had war production machines set up and in operation in Japanese homes all over the city of Hiroshima, Japan. On August 6, 1945, President Truman decided to use the bomb on this military city. The bomb was a powerful weapon and caused great destruction, but Japan still did not surrender. Three days later, President Truman ordered another A-bomb to be dropped on a city similar to Hiroshima by the name of Nagasaki, Japan. Then Japan unconditionally surrendered, ending the war.

By using this weapon and ending the war, President Truman saved hundreds of thousands of lives of our men in the military services and also saved as many Japanese lives. Fortunately, a democratic society had developed and controlled the A-bomb and no territorial demands were made on any other country at the end of the war. If a dictator controlled country had had the A-bomb and used it, they would have attempted to take control of the entire world.

At the end of World War II, rocket, and jet-powered aircraft were developed, and these exceeded the speed of sound.

Harold finally received his drafting orders on August 9, 1945, VJ day—the end of the war. All the men who had just received their notice to report to the U.S.

military service were notified they didn't have to report for duty, since the war was over. Thus, Harold did not have to serve in active duty. By that time Jerry, had been born, and it would have been a real hardship for us if Harold had been away from home.

The home we built had by a hand-fired, coal furnace for heat. Later stokers were designed for home use, and we installed one in our home. A stoker was a large bin that had to be filled daily with coal. The stoker had an auger which automatically fed coal into a special burner in the center of the furnace, and the stoker was controlled by a thermostat to keep the temperature regulated. An attachment to convert furnaces from coal to gas became available, and we replaced the stoker with the gas appliance. This was easier and much cleaner to use than coal, and there were no ashes to remove.

We had a nice sized lot where we grew a garden and canned the vegetables. We also bought fruit and canned it for the winter, making use of the knowledge I acquired when I was growing up. In a few years, home freezers became available, and we purchased a large one from Sears. It was better and quicker to process vegetables for freezing than to can them, and the food had an almost fresh flavor which made this appliance more desirable.

Often, I would make soup in large quantities to freeze. The brand name of our deep freeze was Cold Spot, and we also bought some of their disposable containers, made of cardboard with the name, *Cold Spot*, on them to use for freezing the food. Harold took some vegetable soup to his parents. After his dad ate the soup, he said to Harold, "This soup is the best I've ever eaten. Where is it sold, as I'd like to buy some?" I guess Harold forgot to tell him it was some I had made; I thought it was a great compliment from my father-in-law. Now, frozen foods are available in small packages and can be purchased as needed. Also all kinds of frozen prepared foods and individual meals are sold in the freezers of the stores, as all of you probably know.

During the first year our country was involved in World War II, my dad (age 54) developed a cough. Many people had the flu, and the doctor treated Dad for the flu. The cough persisted all winter, and the doctor finally sent him to a specialist who diagnosed Dad with a severe heart condition. So, by doctor's orders, he was unable to continue to work at Du Ponts. The heart problem was caused from his work in the charcoal mill at Du Ponts where he milled charcoal into dust and mixed it with sulfur to be used in making black powder. This coated his lungs causing him the have *"black lung,"* like the coal miners. His heart had to work harder to compensate for his inability to get enough oxygen from his lungs, and caused his heart to enlarge. Even though Dad wore a muzzle fitted with a moist sponge to act as a filter over his nose and mouth for protection as he breathed, it was not efficient enough to completely eliminate the problem of the dust getting into his lungs. There were no unemployment compensation or sick benefits at that time. This caused a real hardship for my parents.

Through the years Mother had worked hanging wall paper which she was expert at, but the rheumatoid arthritis she was afflicted with had crippled her joints so much she was unable to do that anymore. She felt selling Avon Cosmetic Products, which were well-known and a good product, was a good way to earn extra income. She worked hard and steadily, developing quite a nice big group of customers. The income from this helped but was not enough for their living expenses.

With Dad unable to work anymore at Du Ponts, their income was very limited. Dad was not an idle person, and with a lot of thought about how he could bring in some income, he decided he would learn to operate a loom to weave rag rugs and sell them. This entailed buying a loom and warp and acquiring material from anyone that had cast-off clothing, worn sheets, towels, etc. He cut the good part of these items into strips, sewed them together, and rolled the rags into balls to use for weaving the rugs. From a clothing factory in Keokuk, he obtained material and trimmings left from the cloth cuttings of the merchandise made there. Mother also worked with him, and they made beautiful rag rugs and sold them all over their area. We sold many for them in Peoria. He had customers who cut and sewed their own rags, and then hired Dad to weave their rags into rugs for them. So his venture was successful.

A couple of months ago, I was talking to my son, Jim, and I said, "Jim, you work so hard—all of my children work so hard, and I am concerned about all of you."

He replied, "Well, I don't recall having any lazy ancestors."

My brother, Larry, graduated from high school at age sixteen, and Harold told him and my parents about an apprentice course offered at Caterpillar Tractor Co. Larry thought he would like to try it and he was accepted into the program, but after six months, he left the Co. At age 17, he enlisted in the Navy during World War II. After the war, he obtained a job at the Journal Star as a reporter. Two years later, the Korean War started and he was called back into service. When he was eligible for discharge, he attended the University of Iowa on the G.I. Bill and graduated in three years, with honors, in English. In his senior year, he met Marilyn Lochow, and they married after their graduations. They had three beautiful girls, Laura Lynn, Julia Ann, and Susan Marie, and a handsome son, Laurence Leroy, Jr. After about twenty years, the family split up. A few years later, Larry met and married Nancy Barnes. He went back to college and became an ordained minister in the Lutheran church. Larry and his wife, Nancy, live in Florida, and he continues to serve as a pastor in the Lutheran church.

LIFE WITH CHILDREN

Chapter 7

RELATED HERE ARE SOME OF THE MISHAPS of growing up and also some of the cute and clever (I think) things the children did and said when they were little.

We heard someone whistling, and after investigating, discovered it was Jim. What was unusual about this was Jim was only seven months old. He continued to whistle off and on for several weeks and then forgot about doing it. Jim started talking and making sentences before he was a year old. People that heard him were quite astounded, but I didn't know that it was unusual. Since he was our first child, I had no one to compare him to.

One day when Jim was about two years old, his dad took him on an errand to Wahlfeld's cabinet store in East Peoria. It was the fall before Christmas, and they had some toys there. Jim saw a small wooden dump truck (metal was not available due to the war), and he said, "Daddy, I want that truck." Harold said he couldn't refuse to buy the truck for Jim since that was the first thing Jim ever asked for. Jim loved to be read to. His favorite book was an animated book of Peter Rabbit. He began to know it by heart, and so did I. In later years, I asked him about this book, and he didn't even remember it. I didn't think he'd ever forget it!

Jim was four and was playing in the basement, while I was doing the laundry. When I was outside hanging the clothes on the line, I heard him cry out and ran to see what was the matter. I found he had caught his right hand in the wringer while it was running. He had been able to push on the top of the wringer to keep his arm from being pulled into it, but the palm of his hand was badly bruised and swollen from the roller going around and around. I quickly pushed on the release bar of the wringer to free his hand. The neighbor next door took care of Jerry, while I rushed Jim to the doctor's office. The doctor knew the injured flesh would slough away. He ordered an ointment called "Scarlet Red" and instructed me to change the dressing everyday. It's the only time I ever used that ointment, and I marveled how each day you could see the wound healing. Jim ended up with a bad scar in the palm of his hand but no permanent impairment, which we were very thankful for. Today to eliminate the formation of a scar, the doctor repairs such damaged tissue by performing plastic surgery.

Jerry had two mishaps when he was small resulting in bad lacerations to his face, one while he was riding a tricycle that had lost the handle guard. He upset his tricycle, and the bared handle made a nasty gash under his chin. Another time, he was on his sled coasting down a neighbor's driveway and hit a bare spot. He slid forward, hit the gravel, and ended up with a large scraped area (now known as road rash) on his forehead which bled profusely.

When Jerry was two, his dad took him to see his grandparents in Peoria, and as he got out of the car and turned, he fell on their cement driveway. Every time he was lifted up, he cried as if in pain, and an Xray revealed he had fractured his collar bone. It was difficult keeping his arm in a sling, but eventually it healed.

For Jim's fourth birthday, his dad built him a swing set from four by four wood lumber. He treated the wood to prevent termites and held it in place with cement. He reinforced it with metal braces also held in place by cement. Harold fastened a trapeze bar, rings, and a swing on it, and our children and all the children in the neighborhood enjoyed this swing set. I liked the children to play in our yard, so I knew where they were and what they were doing. It was very durable, and in later years, the people that bought the house hung a porch swing on it. Factory-built swing sets were not on the market then.

Jim 7, Jerry 4, Cheryl 2

We never traveled much, but one summer we decided to go to Minnesota to fish. Harold always liked to fish, and he had discussed this with some of his fellow workers. Through their recommendation, we reserved a cabin for a week on one of the lakes north of St. Cloud, Minnesota, near the little town of Nisswa. On our way, we went through the city of Brainerd where Paul Bunyon is on display and a big attraction. We stopped to view their program which the children enjoyed. Cheryl was quite fascinated by it all, and as the emcee was working on setting up the mikes, she asked, "Daddy, is that Paul Bunyon's little boy?"

The emcee heard her, and after the show, asked her to come up to the stage for an interview. She was always shy but she wasn't shy with him. She went up to him with her daddy and talked to him.

It was a two-day trip each way, and we stayed in a motel one night on our way there and one night on our return. On our way to Minnesota, we found a convenient motel at the crossing of two major highways in Rochester, Minnesota, at a four-way stop intersection. Experience is a good teacher. All night long, the truck traffic stopping for the stop sign, would rev their engines to start up again, and we got very little sleep. (That was before four lane highways and overpasses.) Harold's mother liked to fish, and she went with us—we had a car full. The boys enjoyed the fishing, but it was not much fun for Cheryl as she was only three years old. We made this trip the year before Pamela was born.

After leaving Nisswa, we continued north to Hibbing, Minnesota, to view the mining of the iron ore. It was an open pit mine, and what was so amazing was the depth of the mine and how very tiny the trucking equipment appeared as we viewed it from the visitors' area. The trucks looked like toy vehicles. This is the city where my brother, Marty, went to junior college to study business. We returned by the way of Wisconsin Dells and found a nice motel (not at a four-way stop) to stay in overnight. Wisconsin Dells had been developed into a tourist attraction and featured boat trips on the Dells and an evening of musical entertainment, which we all enjoyed.

Before Pamela was born and Cheryl was about two years old, a friend of mine became interested in plastic products developed and manufactured by a small company in Chicago by the name of Yardley Plastic Company. This company made beautiful material of different colors with floral designs on some of it from plastic. From the materials, the company produced numerous articles, such as bedspreads, curtains, garment bags of all sizes, and raincoats. Material and ruffled trim were sold by the yard for people who liked to sew. A manager for the Peoria area hired unit managers to build a sales group to demonstrate and sell the plastic in the home on a party plan, and my friend decided to try this. She encouraged me to join her unit and try this method of earning extra money part-time. Since we had three small children at the time, I was interested in earning some extra income. I didn't have much confidence in my ability though. I had never done anything like that before, but by my friends having parties for me, it developed into quite a busy time for me. Then my friend was promoted to manager for this area and encouraged me to form a unit of my own. Eventually, I had about 20 women selling plastics, and I became very busy with weekly meetings and training the women before they started on their own. I worked with this about two years, and when my commission check was bigger than the one Harold brought home, he became unhappy instead of glad. I decided I had plenty of work to do caring for my family, so I resigned my position.

When I became involved in selling Yardley Plastic Products by party plan, Harold and I encouraged Mother to try it, as that would help them increase their income. After Mother decided to get the merchandise, Dad helped Mother by driving her to the parties and carrying the suitcases containing the plastic products. Mother demonstrated the products at the parties, took orders, and set up dates for more parties. When the merchandise arrived, Dad helped her sort and deliver it to the hostess who had the party. So by working together, they were able to do this work and became very successful.

A few years later (about 1952, I think), Du Pont closed the plant in Keokuk. The houses the Du Pont employees and retirees were living in were offered to them for a nominal price. My parents were happy about this opportunity, and with the money they were able to save from selling Yardley products, were able to buy the house they were living in. The first thing Dad did, with the help of my brother Marty, was install a bathroom. Finally, in their later years of life, they were able to enjoy the luxury of having indoor plumbing.

We often went to Keokuk to visit my parents. Sometimes other relatives would be visiting there at the same time, because after Mother's parents passed away, her sister and all of her brothers used my parents' home as the "family gathering place." On one of our visits, Mother's sister, Eunice, and husband, Todd, flew from Fort Wayne, Indiana, to Keokuk in a small two-passenger airplane, probably a Taylor Craft. Todd had taken flying lessons, and they decided to rent a plane and fly to Keokuk. The airfield, where small planes could land was a small grass landing area in a farmer's field about eight miles north of Keokuk.

While they were there, we were invited to take a ride in the plane. As the plane only held two people, Todd took Harold and Jim, age five at the time and held by his dad, for a flight over the Mississippi River and back. Then Todd took me, and I held Jerry on my lap. Jerry was only two, and I don't know if he remembers this or not. I was a little apprehensive about flying. My confidence in Todd's pilot ability did not rate too high, but we landed safely, and it was a nice experience. I remember it seemed we were close to the telephone wires when we were landing, and I didn't care for that at all.

On each of the children's birthdays, I baked them a special birthday cake and decorated it with different designs by using a little cake decorator. We always invited the grandparents for dinner to help celebrate their birthdays. On Jim's fourth birthday, Jerry was ten  months old, and as we were doing the dishes in the kitchen, I looked at Jerry and saw him take four steps. I hadn't seen him take even one step before that, so this was a surprise. He was always a very busy little boy and liked to do his own thing. He never wanted me to hold him, but when Cheryl was born, he kept wanting to get on my lap. After he got on my lap, he'd stay about a minute. Jerry still didn't want to be held, but he wanted to be sure he could get on my lap if he wanted to.

I think it was on Jim's seventh birthday that and all of his grandparents were present to help him celebrate. After dinner when we were getting ready to cut his cake, Jim's little neighbor friends came. Jim had invited them to share his birthday cake and ice cream. It was a good thing I had enough for everybody. My mother thought that was cute of Jim to want to share with his friends.

The two boys most always played together. If Jim decided he wanted to go outside and Jerry to go with him, Jerry was very careful to put the toy he was playing with in his drawer so it didn't get lost. He wanted to be able to find it when he was ready to play with it again.

We made many trips to Keokuk with our children to visit my family during the summer months. One of the things I remember most about these trips was the many times the children would ask, "How much farther is it?" No matter how many times they made the trip, it always seemed unbearable for them to be confined in one place for so long. They were such healthy, active children.

Mother and Dad came to Peoria quite often to visit and liked bringing something for the children. One time when Jerry was about three and was playing with a puzzle Mother had brought him, he paused, looked up at her, and said, "Grandma, why didn't you bring me something else?"

She asked, "Jerry, what did you want?"

His answer was, "Just something else." In his estimation, anything would have been better than that puzzle.

Harold worked second shift at Caterpillar, and we didn't get up before eight. One morning Jerry, about three years old, came to my bedside and said, "Mom, get up and cook." That was an original way for him to tell me he was hungry. Direct and to the point.

When Harold worked in the garden, the boys liked to be taken for rides in the wheelbarrow by their dad. As the girls grew big enough, they enjoyed riding in the wheelbarrow, too. When the boys were older, they requested a BB gun. Mothers never want their boys to have them, but are usually overruled by the fathers. So they had BB guns, and this really was a good learning experience for them. It helped them learn how to aim and hit small objects, and they taught their sister to shoot, too. But like all BB guns, they were used in a way they shouldn't have been. The neighbor boy was tormenting them. He probably wanted to join them. I don't remember (maybe I never knew) which one aimed the BB gun at the boy, but Jim or Jerry hit him just about the eye. That put an end to the BB guns. But what a relief it was to learn the boy's eye was not injured

Harold, Jerry & Cheryl

While I was in the hospital and Cheryl was born, Jim was in kindergarten and broke out with chicken pox, thus exposing Jerry. I knew Jerry would also get the chicken pox after our return home and was concerned that Cheryl would contract the disease from him. The doctor assured me Cheryl would be immune to the chicken pox for three months. He was wrong. When she was four weeks old, she had a temperature, and sure enough in a few days, chicken pox. Her attack was mild though. She had only about twelve spots.

Jim was about eight, Jerry five, and Cheryl three, when the terrible *polio epidemic* occurred. This was a scary time. No one knew when someone might get sick with polio which was very crippling and sometimes fatal. Dr. Saulk developed the polio vaccine which rapidly curtailed the spread of the disease. Then Dr. Sabin developed an oral vaccine, and everyone was encouraged to take it, including grandparents. It was given at the schools, and a large percent of the population participated in this program. We were so thankful our family escaped having this dreadful disease.

One year, all the children had infected tonsils and a bad cough. Our doctor called in a prescription of penicillin for me to give to each of them intramuscularly (since I was a nurse and qualified to do this). Jim, being the oldest and elected (by me) to be first, had a terrific fear of needles, and he ran upstairs and hid under the bed. This didn't help him, as he still had to come out from under there and let me give him his medication.  You can imagine after all that, Jerry and Cheryl were absolutely terrified but let me give them their shots, too. They probably knew there was no alternative.

The spring of 1950, a year before Pamela was born, Harold changed jobs, leaving Cat for a position with a company selling pre-need cemetery lots. It was a new concept for a cemetery. Statues representing different themes of the Bible dominated divided areas of the cemetery, eliminating the use of large individual headstones. Flat markers were the only personal stones permitted. It was strictly a commission income position.

The next spring, in 1951, a group of the cemetery personnel and their families were invited to the home of one of the salesmen to watch a television[10] they had just purchased. There were no local stations, and the reception of the picture came from a city about 90 miles away. The program we watched was *I Love Lucy* which we all enjoyed, but the reception was  very snowy, and the picture was sometimes difficult to see clearly. That fall, in 1951, television stations were opened in Peoria, and television reception was immensely improved. Most everyone bought a television if they possibly could. We purchased an RCA and was fortunate it was a good television, requiring very little repair through the years. The children were fascinated with this new form of entertainment in our home Pamela was just a baby when we purchased our first television, but when she was old enough her favorite program was *"Miss Frances"* conducting a school. The program seemed so

Marie, Pamela, Cheryl, Jerry, Jim

real to her, one day she went to the back of the television to see if she could get into the television to join the group. We all enjoyed television. The programs were projected toward family life with many comedy programs. Wonderful movies and musicals produced for television were aired in the evening and contained no violence like they do today, making television viewing enjoyable for the entire family. Even advertising was interesting and not as lengthy or loud as it is today.

    As Pamela grew older, she didn't like to go to bed before the other children, and as soon as she was walking learned how to flip over the side of the crib to get out of bed even with her blanket sleeper on.

    When Pamela was about a month old, Cheryl, on the way home from school, was walking with a little neighbor friend who had just moved to our area from the state of Tennessee. The little girl wanted to see Cheryl's baby sister so they came in, and as the little girl was looking at Pamela, she coughed, and it sounded like she had whooping cough. Sure enough she did, and Pamela came down with whooping cough when she was just a few weeks old. In Peoria, children were immunized against that, but apparently the little girl hadn't been immunized in the area where she was from. Whooping cough is usually fatal to small babies, and Pamela became very sick. I put in an emergency call to the doctor, but he didn't come until afternoon. By that time after caring for her and holding her, she had become better. The doctor ordered an antibiotic for her, and she recovered, but we were very worried about her. Later, I realized I should have rushed her to the hospital. After that, I changed to a doctor I could depend on.

Eventually, we replaced the antiquated sewing machine with a new small portable featherweight Singer sewing machine that provided many years of pleasure. I made dresses for myself, my two darling girls and when Jim and Jerry were small, most of their clothes. For Jim, I made a short pant and jacket suit from one of his dad's discarded wool suits. It was very pretty material and too nice not to be able to use it for something. I also made Jim a little wool coat out of my navy blue nurse's cape. Jerry wore these clothes when he grew to that size. I dressed Cheryl, and later Pamela, in darling little dresses that had to be laundered and ironed. I did not mind doing that because they looked so cute in the little dresses. Sometimes, I made the dresses alike for the girls when they were small. For many years at Halloween time, I sewed costumes for all the children. When Jim was in kindergarten, I made a cat costume for him. He wasn't too fond of it after he wore it to school, because some of the kids at school kept trying to pull on the costume's tail. I made a clown costume all of them wore at different times, an angel costume for Pamela, a cowgirl outfit for Cheryl, and many more I don't seem to remember.

The summer Cheryl was two and a half, new neighbors, Doris and John Quinn, moved next door. They had a new little baby boy, and I went over to greet them. I learned John worked at Cat, and Doris was a nurse, originally from Alton, Illinois. She had been working at Proctor Hospital until her baby was born. We became very good friends, and last year, we celebrated our friendship of 50 years by having our husbands take us out to dinner. Then Doris and I planned an all-day bus trip to a show and luncheon at Rock Island, Illinois. We felt being friends for 50 years was worth a celebration. They had two more children, and we had one more.

Doris graduated from a nursing school in Alton, Illinois. Since her school was out of town, I invited Doris to join my Proctor Alumnae Association as an associate member, and she accepted. During our years as members, we shared being hostess to many Alumnae banquets and picnics. Doris is a great party planner and known for her fun parties. One year for the banquet, Doris suggested I make small student nurse uniforms, a duplicate of the uniforms we wore when we were in training at Proctor, and dress little dolls in them for door prizes. Doris had never to learned to sew, but she knew I sewed a lot. At first, I didn't think I could do that but after thinking about it, I decided to try. I made uniforms for 10 dolls. These were so well received, I had requests for more and decided to make an additional 10 as a fund raising project for the alumnae. Since the dolls were so attractive, I made one for each of my granddaughters. Doris and I always planned something special, and our parties were always a big success.

When I worked at private duty on a long case, Doris relieved me by working in my place when I wanted time off. She also worked as a relief nurse at Hiram Walkers occasionally when one of the regular nurses couldn't report for duty.

We have shared many activities over the years. Some of our projects were quite big. For a number of years, one project involved baking dinner rolls and pecan rolls from five lbs. of flour a piece, which we froze to enjoy later. Another activity we enjoyed together was taking short overnight bus trips sponsored by our bank. We have enjoyed many years of playing bridge and golf together. A true friend is a treasure.

There was a little girl about four, the same age as Cheryl, in the neighborhood, and they played together. One problem the little girl had was a bad habit of biting if she didn't get what she wanted. After the third time she bit Cheryl, I complained to the little girl's mother, but she seemed unconcerned about it. One afternoon, Cheryl was riding her tricycle at another neighbor's home and came home crying. That little girl has been there too, and had sunk her teeth real hard in the left cheek of Cheryl's buttock leaving a large bruise and teeth marks. She wanted to ride Cheryl's tricycle. Well, I was very upset, and the only solution I could think of was not to let Cheryl play with her anymore. I explained that to her mother, but she was still unconcerned about it. Soon after that, I learned the little girl bit her dad, and he took care of the problem—she never bit anyone again.

Since our home was rather small, as our family grew, we finished the attic into another bedroom and bathroom. Large fans that fit into windows were being manufactured for cooling a house, and we purchased one for the upstairs room. The fan had a switch control, enabling it to pull air into the room, or it could be reversed, blowing the air out, making the room comfortable at night. I always picture this home, filled with our family, with the sides of the house bulging.

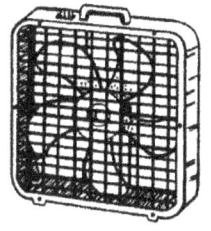

After living there ten years, automatic washers and dryers were available for home use, and we purchased these appliances. Unbelievable almost—that these machines worked so well, and it certainly made an improvement for me on laundry day with a family of six. Special soap was created to make these appliances efficient. At this time, dishwashers for home use had not been designed.

Harold, as a young lad, had a paper route, and when Jim was old enough, Harold encouraged him to get a paper route. Jim applied and was issued a paper route in our area which he serviced several years. When Jerry was old enough, Jim split the route with Jerry, and they took care of it together. Harold helped the children on their route during bad or severely cold weather. Harold taught them to be conscientious and to took good care of their customers. The fall Jim entered high school, he turned the paper route over to Jerry, and sometimes Cheryl helped Jerry on his route. Jerry serviced the route until he entered high school. When Jerry gave up the route, he received many compliments from his customers on the good service they had received from both boys, and all were sorry Jerry was leaving them.

Cheryl and Pamela took dancing lessons when they were small, and I always made the costumes for their recitals. Pamela and her friends enjoyed playing dress-up in the costumes afterward. Cheryl took tap dancing one year, and Pamela took baton twirling. For several years, Pamela marched with the band and twirled her baton in parades in Peoria. She remembers how cold it was sometimes and how skimpy the costumes were. Baton twirling isn't as easy as it looks. When Pamela was first learning, her arms were covered with bruises for several weeks before she learned how to handle the baton.

At an early age, Cheryl revealed her talent for sewing which was quite impressive. When she was about five years old, one of the little neighbor girls had a birthday. Cheryl, free-hand, cut out a little doll from white muslin, sewed it together, and stuffed it with cotton. Then she embroidered a face on it and made a dress and little hat for it. She didn't ask for any help, except for me to thread her needle. It was a beautiful little doll, and I would like to have kept it, but she gave it to the little girl for her birthday.

Cheryl was a little gardener and enjoyed helping the neighbor pull weeds in his garden. She also helped her grandpa Koss in his garden when she was visiting her grandparents.

When Cheryl was old enough, I taught her how to sew on the sewing machine. At age twelve, Cheryl read about the Singer Sewing Machine Co.'s sewing contest for preteens, teens, and adults, and she wanted to enter it. To enter, the contestant was required to take sewing lessons at the Singer Co.'s place of business. We signed her up for the lessons, enabling her to enter the contest in the preteen group. As she was sewing, she became enthused about the new automatic sewing machines at Singers with built-in attachments. This interested me also, and we decided we'd trade in my little portable Singer for one of the new models, enabling me to blind hem and do all kinds of fancy stitches with it. I have used this machine and made many beautiful things ever since. For the contest, Cheryl made a pretty cotton dress and received honorable mention in the preteen local division.

At age 14, Cheryl decided to enter the sewing contest again. She made a beautiful three-piece wool suit, won the contest in the local division of the teen group, and received an overnight suitcase. The Singer personnel were impressed with her sewing ability and encouraged her to enter again the following year.

Cheryl thought about it for awhile and decided to try the contest again. This time she made a stunning full-length prom dress of white satin with turquoise satin trim. The feature of this dress was a long stole, lined in the turquoise satin with trapunto trimming along one side of it, which was attached to the right shoulder of the dress. When worn, the stole draped over the other shoulder and hung to about three quarters length of the dress. The trimming was made by machine using very small stitches with turquoise thread along the edges of a design traced onto the material with white marking chalk (difficult to see and follow). The inside of the design was stuffed with yarn giving the design a raised look, creating quilted embroidery.

This dress won the local division and also the regional division. From the local division, Cheryl received another overnight case, which she gave to me, and I treasured. The United States was divided in five regions, and for the regional prize, she received a new model portable Singer sewing machine. Her dress was sent to New York City for judging, the prize for that was a trip to Paris. The dress was gone a long time, and we became worried about it, but eventually it was returned. Cheryl didn't win the trip and was disappointed, but she was honored and very happy with her new sewing machine.

Since the war, nurses were in short supply, and I was contacted by Proctor Hospital for employment. I worked part-time as a float nurse on the night shift for about a year (by that time nurses worked an eight-hour shift). Then I became pregnant with Pamela and didn't work for another four years.

Harold selling for the cemetery on commission made our income varied and sometimes meager, and I started work at Methodist Hospital on the second shift as a med. nurse (dispensing medications to the patients). Harold was home in the evenings with the children. I worked about six months when Harold left the cemetery company and returned to Cat on third shift. This meant he had to 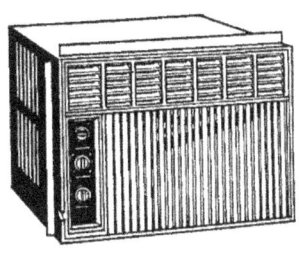 sleep days, which was not a good situation in the summertime when the children were home from school. We took the bedroom upstairs, and at this time, window air conditioners for a home were available. Harold picked out a York, which was made by a well-known company who had been in the air-conditioning business for public buildings and offices for some time. (It was a good choice and was used for many years. We took it to Champaign for Jim when he returned to college to study for his master's degree. At this time he was married with a family of three children. After Jim completed his degree and before they moved back to Los Alamos, Jim and his dad installed the air conditioner in the window of Cheryl's small upstairs apartment. When she moved from that apartment, the air conditioner was left there; it gave long and good service.)

Since Harold was working third shift, I went back to private duty nursing on the day shift. Because I was self-employed, I could stay home in the summer when the children were not in school. Pamela was four years old, and I contacted the church we attended, First Methodist Church of East Peoria, to inquire if there was someone I could hire take care of Pamela while I worked. Our minister's wife, Mrs. Coulter, said she would like to take care of her. Her children were all in high school, and she liked the idea of having a little-one to enjoy. This was wonderful. She was like a second mother to Pamela, and I knew she was well taken care of.

All my patients were special to me, and sometimes they asked me to care for them in their home after leaving the hospital. One of my patients I had taken care of in her home passed away after a long terminal illness. Sometimes, I had driven my patient on errands, using her automobile, if she felt well enough. While I took care of her, she insisted I use her automobile for transportation instead of riding the bus. After her death, the surviving family told me they would like to give me her automobile if I felt we'd like to have a second car. This was a wonderful gift, and we were very thankful. This helped in many ways. I didn't have to take the bus to work anymore and Jim, who had just received his driver's license, helped transport the other children to their different activities. The automobile was a Buick with less than 10,000 miles on it and in mint condition. I don't remember how old it was, but I think it was about four years.

About a year later, another older member of their family fell and broke her hip, and I was engaged to take care of her. This lady developed problems with her memory and when she was able to leave the hospital, I was retained to care for her in her home. Since nurses only worked an eight-hour shift, three nurses were employed to care for her around the clock. I worked the 7 to 3 shift, and took care of her for ten years.

The year Harold started back to Cat on third shift, we were unable to decide what to get Jerry for his birthday. We thought we would give him money and let him pick out something he especially wanted. I was working, and Harold said he would take Jerry shopping after he came home from work. Harold ate breakfast and when the stores opened (at 9:00 a.m.), he took Jerry to Peoria. After going to many stores and trying to decide what to spend his money on, Jerry very hesitantly asked his dad, "Dad, do you care if I don't buy anything?" Harold said he couldn't get upset if Jerry didn't buy something if he didn't find anything he wanted.

When Jim was a sophomore in high school, we built a larger home with an attic fan that cooled our house sufficiently. The air conditioner was installed in our bedroom window and used during the daytime while Harold was sleeping. (He remained on third shift when we moved to our new home.) Our new home was a beautiful brick ranch and nice and roomy for our large family. After having the basement dug, Harold laid the cement blocks for our basement with Jerry's help. Jerry was 14 years of age, and he mixed and carried all the mortar for building the basement during his summer vacation. This gave us a nice start on our new home. Harold contracted the rest of the construction to different journeymen after inspecting their work on other homes they had worked on; thus, we saved the expense of a contractor. We moved into our new home the following February in 1958.

We had been in our new home about five years, and automatic dishwashers were beginning to be perfected and marketed. We purchased one and enjoyed using it even though Jim and Jerry were away at school and our family was smaller. A dishwasher sterilizes, the dishes making them more sanitary than when the dishes are washed by hand. This helps to prevent colds and flu from spreading through the family, if a member of the household is ill. I'm a firm believer in dishwashers.

We bought Pamela a bicycle for her eighth birthday. She was so thrilled with her new bike, she spent all day learning to ride it and was determined to conquer it. She ended the day, having mastered riding it, but she had one mass of bruises on her legs and arms. It took me longer than one day to learn to ride a bike.

Pamela had a little friend, Lynn, whose mother was very ill and in the hospital. Lynn wanted to make a dress to show her mother, and Pamela asked me if I would help. The three of us went shopping for material and a pattern, and I taught Lynn and Pamela both to sew, making their dresses with the same pattern. When Lynn wore her dress to visit her mother, her mother was very proud of her. A few months later Lynn's mother died, and I was glad to have been able to help Lynn accomplish her desire. Several years later, after Lynn had married, she stopped by our home to show me the maternity outfit she was wearing—one she had made and to thank me for teaching her to sew. Little do we realize how much younger people retain or how, in some ways, we sometimes influence their lives.

Pamela enjoyed sewing but wasn't interested in entering a contest. When Pamela was in high school and needed a prom dress, she picked one out of the *Seventeen* magazine she would like to have and asked me if I could make one like it for her. I went shopping, found a pattern I could adapt, and bought the material to make a dress very similar to the one she wanted. The dress was made of beautiful sheer pink material and lined with matching satin. I found matching Irish lace designs to appliqué on the bodice. Through the years, both of my daughters have made many of their own clothes. Now

Cheryl has a great time making little clothes for her grandchildren.

All the children had their own bicycles and took swimming lessons at the Y. One day Jerry was swimming at the East Peoria pool, and just as he dove into the water, Cheryl's friend, Lindy, began to surface right under him. He landed on the top of her head. <u>OUCH</u>! Jerry didn't tell me about it, but the next day, I could see his nose was swollen and ask him about it. He told me what happened. I took him to the doctor and an Xray confirmed his nose was broken. Later I learned, Lynn had suffered a terrific headache from the accident, which was understandable.

The children were all active in scouting and enjoyed spending a week in the summer at scout camp and attending numerous overnight special events at the camps. Cheryl had a very good scout leader who encouraged her to work for the Circle Bar awarded to Girl Scouts, which is equivalent to the Eagle award for Boy Scouts. Cheryl worked on many projects and received her Circle Bar award. Pamela received many patches for Girl Scouts but not enough for the Circle Bar. Now I think the name has been changed to the Gold Award for Girl Scouts.

One thing we enjoyed for many years as a family was an all-day outing at Pekin park every 4th of July. The children swam, followed by a picnic, and the evening ended with an entertainment program and a beautiful display of fireworks in the stadium. Most of my children have carried on this tradition with their families. We usually took the same menu: fried chicken, baked beans, cold slaw, sliced tomatoes, potato chips, and apple pie. (But their menu has probably changed to green chili burgers, guacamole dip with corn chips, and taco salad.)

Sometimes we would ask another family with children to go with us.

When Jim graduated from eighth grade, he asked for an Amateur Radio Handbook as he was interested in radio and wanted to become a member of the Ham Radio Club. This was entirely a new field for me, but we supported Jim in his interest. He studied all summer, with the goal of passing a written test and a code test. When he had mastered the code and studied all the material, he asked me to take him to a Radio Shop on S. Adams St. in Peoria. Jim had an appointment with the owner who was licensed to give the tests. I was somewhat concerned, as the shop was not in a very good area of Peoria, so I stayed right there until Jim had completed all the tests. As I became acquainted with the owner and his wife, who helped take care of the business, I found they were very nice people. I appreciated the interest they took in my Jim and also in my Jerry when he became involved in Ham Radio. Jim passed, received his license, and has enjoyed this hobby all through the years, although he doesn't have much time for it now.

Jerry and Jim always spent a lot of time together, and a couple of years later, with Jim's encouragement, Jerry also became a Radio Ham. Like Jim, he studied and practiced the code and took and passed the tests, given by the same people Jim had gone to for his tests. They spent many hours together contacting people all over the world. Jerry received call cards from Hams in every state and many foreign countries. These cards were traded with the ham operator after a radio contact was made.

Jim built a power supply and a special table for their equipment in their *ham shack* (this is what they called their radio room) in the basement of our new home. The boys spent many hours working with their radios and studying electronics in their *ham* shack. Jim and Jerry had several friends who were Hams, and they enjoyed spending time with them in the *ham shack*.

After Jim became a Ham, he built a portable radio from a Heath Kit. Jerry also built a Heath Kit portable radio after he became a Ham. This was a good project advised by the Radio Store, and it helped the boys to utilize what they had learned. It proved to be a very valuable hobby and provided a good background for their futures, Jim became a physicist, and Jerry became an electronic technician. With this knowledge, Jerry learned about computers and has worked in that field for many years.

Jim and Jerry have continued to use their Ham Radio, especially the portable ones they have for traveling. The radio has been very useful in many ways—for asking directions when traveling through a strange city or looking for a store or some special area in particular, like a park for the children to play in for awhile. They find it useful when traveling in a group to check on the whereabouts of the other automobiles. They have also used it to radio for help when coming upon an accident or for someone stranded on the mountain roads.

Two different summers we were invited to Fort Wayne, Indiana, to visit my Aunt Eunice and her husband, Howard, (she had remarried), Stan, her son, and Buddy, her grandson. With us were Jerry, Cheryl, and Pamela. From Fort Wayne, we followed Eunice and her family to their cottage on Wall Lake in northeastern Indiana. The children enjoyed the swimming and fishing in the lake, and we all had a great time. One day we went on an outing to Lake Michigan to see the dunes and go swimming in Lake Michigan. We had a large Nash Sedan and it was quite roomy. I really hate to tell you how many of us went in the car, but I will. In the front seat sat two adults, one child in the center, and one child held by Howard. In the back seat sat two adults, and two children on the seat, and I held Pamela. Did you count? That was a total of nine people. The children were well-behaved, but that many in

an auto is illegal now. On our way, Eunice told us about a drive-in located in Fort Wayne where they had good hamburgers, and just as she was talking about it, she said, "Oh stop, there is one of those hamburger places." Can you guess what it was? Yes, it was one of the first McDonald's. It was about two o'clock and with little business at that time of day, they had no burgers prepared. They took our order and cooked them while we waited. I've never tasted any hamburgers that good at McDonald's since. We really appreciated Aunt Eunice and Uncle Howard's invitation to us. When one has a large family, not too many invitations are issued to you.

  The summer my dad was 72 years of age, he began to have severe health problems, but his doctor didn't seem to help him The latter part of August, his breathing became difficult, and his doctor arranged for him to be hospitalized. I went to Keokuk and stayed nights with him for a week. I had two cousins in Keokuk, who were nurses, Aunt Lena's older daughters, and they also stayed with him in the daytime. They were very fond of their Uncle Martin. His condition did not improve, but I had to return home since Jim was getting ready to leave for his first year of college, and I needed to help him. A few days later, I returned to Keokuk and went directly to the hospital. By this time Dad's condition was much worse, and he died shortly after I arrived there. The autopsy showed multiple blood clots had formed in his heart and lungs, hindering his oxygen supply.

After the funeral, Mother stayed with us for about a month. She liked to talk about how she baked cookies for us and the boys and their friends in the *ham shack* made many trips through the kitchen, picking up freshly baked cookies on their way. It made her feel good for them to swipe her cookies. After she returned to her home, she continued to live there alone for 14 years. Marty and Leola and I helped her maintain her home by doing things for her which she was unable to do. Mother continued to make rugs and have a good business with them. She had stopped selling plastic a few years before Dad passed away.

The beginning of the *space age*[11] was about 1958 when Russia and the United States began developing programs to place people in earth orbit. In 1969, the goal of a moon landing was achieved, with millions of people witnessing the event on television. What a thrill to watch this while it was actually taking place.

LEAVING THE NEST

Chapter 8

UPON GRADUATING FROM HIGH SCHOOL, Jim learned he was twelfth in his class. He received a scholarship from the Rotary Club of East Peoria and a tuition scholarship to many colleges. His choice was the University of Illinois because it had a good reputation as an engineering school. The first year Jim was in college, he needed to work part-time to supplement his living expenses. He started working in the cafeteria at the Delta Tau Delta Fraternity House where he lived and was a member. He decided that kind of work was not for him and applied for work at the WILL radio station in Champaign. He was told he needed an FCC license. Jim told them he'd go to Chicago that weekend and take the required test for one. Were they surprised when Jim returned with his license. They thought he would have to study first; they didn't realize how much he knew about radio. Jim got the job and worked there until he graduated. In college, Jim was on the Dean's list, a James Scholar, and active in the Physics Club.

    While Jim was in his senior year at the University of Illinois, the job recruiters from the Research Lab in Los Alamos, New Mexico, interviewed him for a position with their lab. They furnished airfare and lodging for Jim to visit their lab and receive further interviewing. None of us knew anything about the state of New Mexico, and this was a traveling experience for Jim. He was interested in employment there and accepted their offer. He wrote many interesting letters to us about his impressions of the New Mexico land formations.

Jim didn't date very much while in college. Not having an automobile to use made dating difficult. When Jim was a senior, we gave him some money for graduation, and he made a down payment on an automobile. About this time, a friend introduced Jim to a very pretty young lady, Darlene Danz, who lived in Peoria. He made many trips from Champaign to Peoria to see her, and they became engaged toward the end of his senior year. Darlene is very talented, quite musical, enjoys playing the piano, and singing, and is active in the community plays and musicals in Los Alamos. Upon receiving his B.S. degree at the University of Illinois in January, Jim went to Los Alamos to start his new job. He returned to Peoria for his wedding to Darlene at St. Andrews Church on August 29, 1964. Jim and Darlene have five children—two daughters, Kristin Marie and Anna Louise, a son, Rudolf Harold, known as Rudy, and two adopted sons, John Scott and Greg James. They also had an infant daughter that was stillborn.

After graduation, Jim continued to work with one of the professors at the college, Dr. Frauenfelder, on his Ph.D. project. He wrote his thesis titled *The Parity Violations and Proton-Proton Scattering*. Jim gave me a copy of his thesis, but I must confess, I really had a difficult time trying to understand it.

Jim was on the staff at the lab for 20 years. He made many trips to Europe, consulting with labs in Germany, Switzerland, and France, and he became well-known for his expertise as an accelerator physicist. After 20, Jim left his job at the Lab, and he and three other scientists joined forces and started their own business. They were together eight years and started having business disagreements. Jim and one other of the four decided to leave the company. Jim has formed his own company, *Jim Potter Accelerator Works*, working an a consulting basis and developing new projects on his own.

After Jerry graduated from high school, he entered the U.S. Air Force for a term of three years. Jerry had been afflicted with headaches occasionally, and when he was taking basic training his headaches turned into full fledged migraines. He was treated in the base hospital but was unable to get permanent relief. After four months, he received an honorable medical discharge.

Upon Jerry's return home, I took him to our family doctor who stated that migraine headaches were a hereditary condition. After being questioned by the doctor, I realized the sick headaches my mother's sister, Annabelle, suffered from were migraines, but were never called that. Our doctor was very knowledgeable, and he ordered a prescription for Jerry that alleviated his headaches. Instructions were to take the medication at the very onset to prevent the headache from becoming severe. By following instructions, Jerry was able to control his headaches and rarely has them anymore.

Encouraged by her friend, Lindy, Cheryl joined Job's Daughters. Since Harold belonged to the Masonic Organization, Cheryl was eligible to become a Job's Daughter. There, she was very active and made many friends. One of her friends was Susan Balcom who was also very active. Both became officers and climbed the ladder to become Princesses. On one occasion when Job's Daughters was sponsoring a chicken noodle dinner, Jerry attended, and Cheryl introduced him to Susan, a very pretty girl. They soon began to date. Cheryl had been dating a friend of Jerry's, Paul Hammond, also a ham radio operator, and they had many great times together as a foursome. Jerry bought a small turquoise Metropolitan convertible, which gave them a lot of enjoyment until he sold it when he went away to school.

After returning home from the service, Jerry found employment at L.R. Nelson Mfg. Co. where lawn sprinklers are manufactured, and he worked there a few months. Interested in electronics, Jerry decided he would like to study in that field and enrolled at DeVry Technical School in Chicago that fall. He graduated with honors in January 1965 with a degree in electronic technology. He acquired a position with a small radio shop in Peoria where he worked for a year. While Jerry was away at school, Susan attended Bradley University to studying business. That summer, Jerry and Sue were married June 12, 1965, in the Arcadia Presbyterian Church in Peoria. They have two children, a son, Kenneth Douglas, and a daughter, Cheri Lynn.

Jerry was interested in the Los Alamos lab where his brother Jim was employed. Jim encouraged Jerry to apply for employment, and Jerry was hired. So I had two sons with their families in New Mexico. We made many trips to New Mexico over the years by train, plane, and automobile—every way but by bus or hitchhiking. Since they both married lovely Peoria girls, their families also made many trips to New Mexico.

Sue worked in the office for the lab after their children were in school and has been there many years. Jerry and Sue like dogs and have enjoyed them over the years, training them in obedience. They became members in a dog club, and their dogs earned many trophies and awards at shows all over the country. They found having a motor home to travel and stay in at the various shows made participating in the shows more enjoyable. As a family, they have also used their motor home for extensive traveling. One year, when they came to Illinois, I traveled back to New Mexico with them. It certainly was a fun trip. They knew how to locate good RV parks and planned ahead for places to stay.

Cheryl and Paul continued to date, and after Cheryl's junior year in high school, they eloped to South Carolina. I was very unhappy about her doing that, but I did get Cheryl to promise that she would finish her senior year and graduate from high school, which she did. After getting married, Cheryl could no longer continue in the Job's Daughter organization and was not eligible to fulfill the office of princess.

We had planned to make our first trip to New Mexico that summer with Pamela and Cheryl to see Jim who had moved there and was working at his new job at the lab in Los Alamos. Since Cheryl was in South Carolina with Paul, she didn't get to make the trip with us. On our trip to New Mexico, we planned to bring Darlene back to Illinois with us. She had gone out there the week before to visit Jim and see the area. Jim and Darlene were engaged and planned to be married in a couple of months and make their home there.

On our return home, we stopped in Fort Worth, Texas to visit Harold's aunt Flora, her husband, uncle Jack, and their family. We were there about three days, and we certainly had a good time with everyone. It was our first trip west, and it was very interesting to see the completely different terrain and foliage after we passed through the western side of Missouri.

In the spring, Cheryl and Paul had a baby boy named Dale Allen, our first grandchild. Paul was enrolled in an apprentice course at Caterpillar Tractor Co. to become an electrician. His earnings were meager, and it was a difficult struggle for them.

After Paul completed his apprentice course, Cheryl felt the need to continue her education. In the spring of 1967, Cheryl learned a referendum had been passed by the state of Illinois to build a junior college in East Peoria. She called for an application the next day before the buildings had started to be erected. She was accepted and started in the fall when the school opened. The buildings were temporary government barracks, but they were adequate until the more permanent ones were built. Cheryl took basic requirement courses, and from a friend she had met at the college, learned a nursing program had been started there.

They had purchased a nice little home, and Cheryl was a good little homemaker and cook. But both were so young when they married, the marriage ended in divorced after five years.

After she found an apartment for Dale and herself, she visited me and said, "Mother, I know I have to have more education and have given this a lot of thought. I learned the new Central Illinois College is offering a two-year nursing program for an associate nursing degree, and I have decided I want to become a nurse. I can work part-time and go to school part-time. It will take longer, but in the end I'll be able to make a living to take care of Dale and myself."

I answered, "This really amazes me as you have never expressed this desire before, but it is a wonderful profession with many fields to choose from, and I know, if this is what you want to do, you'll be one of the very best." (And she is.)

The summer of her freshman year of high school, Cheryl had been a candy striper at Proctor Hospital, so she had been exposed to hospitals. This was a volunteer program offered by the hospitals during the summer for high school students to assist with patients.

That fall, Cheryl was accepted into the nursing program. Her sewing skills were helpful to her when she was going to college to become a nurse. She needed part-time work to help with her expenses and was hired for 20 hours a week in the alteration department of a major department store in Peoria. She had been frying tenderloins at Hunt's Drive Inn but liked alterations much better, and the pay was better.

She enrolled Dale in a nursery during the week, and I volunteered to take care of him on Saturdays. I was working full-time and only free on weekends. Cheryl paid her own way, and we helped her by providing her with an automobile for her transportation. She accomplished her goal four years later, graduated with an associate's degree, passed her state board exam, and became a registered nurse in the state of Illinois.

After working in private duty for many years, I decided to try something different. The Red Cross was advertising for staff nurses, and I applied and was accepted. It entailed a lot of traveling with the blood mobile, and many times, it was very late when we returned home. I worked there about two years, but I was having a lot of problems in my marriage, and I left the Red Cross and stayed home. About six months later, Hiram Walker Distillery needed a nurse, and one of my neighbors recommended me to their First Aid Department. I was contacted three times by their charge nurse, asking if I would be interested in applying for the position on second shift. Harold was still working at Caterpillar on second shift, and Pamela was in her third year of high school, so I decided it might be worth looking into. That was the best decision I had made in a long time.

After I had worked at Hiram Walkers about two years, my marriage was terminating and we parted in 1969. Harold drank for many years and became an alcoholic. During those years, I lived in an emotional and sometimes physically abusive relationship. At that time there was no help for a woman in that type of situation, and with the Lord's help, I coped the best I could. Pamela was in college, and I finally knew I could not live that way any longer and decided to leave. It was a very difficult decision for me to make. We had had counseling, but the root of the problem was never addressed in a positive way.

We sold our beautiful home, and with my half of the sale, I was able to make a down payment on a smaller new brick ranch home in a new development in East Peoria. It had a dishwasher and disposal but no air conditioning. After I lived there a couple of years, I had central air conditioning installed, and I made this my home for 20 years. Harold moved in with his parents in the home he grew up in. He was from a family that had a history of drinking. Little did I know about that kind of thing. When someone in my family wanted a drink, it meant they were thirsty for a drink of water. I learned when anyone in Harold's family wanted a drink, they meant an alcoholic beverage. However, I was very fond of my in-laws, and they were always good to me and my children.

By this time, Pamela had completed one year of college at Illinois Central College located in East Peoria.

She had been active in the drama department in high school and had roles in several plays. She also participated and acted in plays given and directed by the college.

Before she entered her second year of college, Pamela became interested in studying interior decorating, and her counselor recommended Ames, Iowa. She made plans to attend school there the next fall and applied and enrolled in Ames College in June. For the summer, Pamela obtained a job at Bergner's Department Store where she represented her school in a program in which Bergner's employed college students to model and sell clothing. Pamela was given the clothes she modeled, and with those clothes and the many sweaters I knitted for her and wool skirts I made to match, she had a very nice wardrobe for college. That fall, I took Pamela and helped her get settled at Ames College which is about 300 miles west of Peoria. This was quite a difficult trip for me alone.

Pamela was not happy with the curriculum at Ames, and after she was there about six weeks, she called Ken Hughes and asked him to come and get her. She had been going with Ken a couple of years, having met him while he was going to college at Bradley University, in Peoria. He had graduated the past spring and was in the navy stationed at the Navy Pier in Chicago. Ken took Pamela to Chicago to his parents' home, and they were married in the Episcopal Church in Chicago. They rented an apartment in Evanston, Illinois, and Pamela enrolled in a college in Chicago where she completed a semester studying interior decorating. She realized interior decorating was not something she wished to make a career of and did not continue that curriculum.

Ken desired to get his master's degree in city management, and Pamela decided she'd like to become a nurse. I had never dreamed my two daughters would become nurses, but it certainly made me proud, and I felt I must have been a good role model and a credit to my profession. There was a good nursing program at Northern Illinois University in DeKalb and a good program for Ken to obtain his master's degree in city management. They moved to DeKalb, and Pamela went to college while Ken completed his service in the navy, going to DeKalb on weekends and whenever he had any other free time. Then he enrolled full time in DeKalb, and they both graduated with honors from DeKalb the spring of 1974, Ken with an M.A. in city management and Pamela with a B.S. degree in nursing.

After graduating from college, they moved to Carpentersville, Illinois, where Ken was employed as an assistant city manager. Pamela found employment in the emergency room at St. Joseph Hospital in Elgin, about 30 miles south of Carpentersville. A couple of years later, they decided to move to New Mexico and settled in Albuquerque. About two years after they moved there, they had a boy, Brian Ivor, and two years later a girl, Joy Elaine. Now, all but one of my four children lived in New Mexico.

LIVING ALONE

Chapter 9

ABOUT A YEAR AFTER MY DIVORCE, I felt I needed some outside activity and learned there was an organization in Peoria for singles called the *Quadrant Club* that held a dance with a live band every week. I had always wanted to be able to ballroom dance, and after searching for a reliable dance studio, a lady friend and I enrolled and learned to ballroom dance. We were taught the *Fox-Trot, Swing,* and *Waltz,* and continued our lessons to learn the Latin dances. Of those, we enjoyed the *Rumba, Cha Cha,* and *Tango* the most. That was another "best decision" as it gave me an activity with a mixed group that was friendly, and we had many outings together as a group. We enjoyed going to dinner dances and dancing to all the big dance bands, like *Wayne King, Guy Lombardo, Al Pierson,* and many others when they came to this area. We also made many trips to the big ballroom at Willow Brook near Chicago and once to the Aragon in Chicago, which had been refurbished, and was promoting a big band dance. After I learned to dance, I attended the *Quadrant Club* and have enjoyed it for many years.

      The game of bridge had interested me for a long time, and by studying a bridge book and with the patience of my friends and encouragement from my special friend,

Doris Quinn, I learned how to play bridge. I am blessed with many bridge friends, and we have many enjoyable days together pursuing that activity.

In my church, I am active in the Phillip Ministry, visiting older members of our church who live in a sheltered care facility. Another activity I pursued was taking instructions to become a literacy teacher, and I had the pleasure of helping many people to improve their reading ability.

After Cheryl graduated from college, she wanted to take me to Spain to the Coastal Del Sol resort area for a 10 day tour sponsored by the college. So we went. We saw the rock of Gibraltar and went to Morocco, crossing the Mediterranean on a large transport boat. We stayed in Tangiers for a couple of days and shopped in the Casbah, which is a maze of little shops on a hillside, where we could easily have been lost without a guide. We toured the country in Africa on a bus and were taken to see some camels. We could get on one for a fee, if we so desired. I have a picture of Cheryl on a camel, but I declined since it was no easy trick to get up on one, even with help. The guide spoke English quite well and after our tour, he said to me, "I want to buy your daughter, I will give you fifty camels for her."

I didn't know what I'd do with fifty camels, so I answered, "No, my daughter is not for sale, as she is a treasure to me." (Later I learned camels were supposedly worth $10,000, but of course Cheryl is worth more to me than half a million dollars. Anyway, Cheryl wasn't interested in becoming a Moroccan.)

We also went to Granada, Spain, an all-day bus tour through a rural mountainous area, where we noted living and farming were very primitive. We went on a Monday, and on our way, our guide pointed out the laundry facilities. Groups of women were doing their laundry in a large tub of water used for watering animals. After scrubbing the clothes, they hung them on the nearby shrubs to dry. Men and women worked the fields by hand with the aid of a pack mule to carry their equipment. Cork trees were grown in that area, and we were told the bark, which is the cork, was stripped from the trees once every eight years. It took that long for the tree to replenish its bark.

The purpose of the trip was to tour the Alhambra, an elaborate estate with a castle built by the Moors after they captured Spain about the year 1300 AD. The Moors were finally driven out of Spain, and the castle remained as a landmark and tourist attraction. It impressed me how fragile a person's life is, and yet some material things can remain intact for hundreds of years. Also in Granada was the church where the crypts of Queen Isabella and King Ferdinand could be viewed by visitors, including us. In April 1492, Queen Isabella and King Ferdinand agreed to sponsor Christopher Columbus on his expedition to sail west to find Asia. Of course you know, he discovered the American continent instead. We had a glorious time with the college group. It was my first trip abroad which I had never contemplated being able to do.

That fall, after our trip, Cheryl married Clifford Richter on May 4, 1973. He was a mechanical engineer employed at Caterpillar, and was from Athens, Illinois. They built a house in Chillicothe, Illinois, about 25 miles north of Peoria. About a year later, through the Lutheran agency, they took a little boy, Bert, to adopt. Bert was born December 29, 1965, in Swan River, Manitoba, Canada. In very bad weather in the early part of December, Cheryl, Cliff, and Dale made a trip to Canada to pick him up and bring him to Illinois. Bert is about a year younger than Dale, and at the same time they adopted Bert, Cliff adopted Dale, too. Now his name is Dale Allen Richter. Bert always says he is a "mail-order kid."

Two years later, in 1977, Cheryl and Cliff had a little girl of their own, Johanna Marie, and another little girl, Heidi Lynne, was born two after that. Cheryl said she thought with me already having so many grandchildren, I would not have any love left for, or care about, any new ones. But she found that I had lots of love and attention for each new grandchild. They all are precious to me. All told, I have thirteen beautiful grandchildren and one lost stillborn.

The summer of 1974, Mother sold her home and moved into an apartment in Keokuk. Mother was very crippled with rheumatoid arthritis, but since she wanted to be independent, she managed to live there even though she had to use a wheelchair the last two years for mobility. Mother had the help of a health care aide, who came five days of the week for a couple of hours each day to help her, and that enabled Mother to stay in her apartment alone. Marty and Leola visited her every other Sunday and did her shopping for her. Leola took her laundry home to do it, so Mother was well cared for. Living so far away, I was unable to help her much in that way, but I was able to provide the health care aide for her every Saturday by paying her wages for that day.

Sometime during a Saturday night, Mother fell and couldn't get up. Marty and Leola went there after church the next day, and finding her on the floor, called an ambulance to take her to the hospital. Fortunately, Mother did not break any bones, but she was kept in the hospital a few days for observation.

We all knew Mother could no longer live alone in her apartment, and Marty knew it would not be easy to persuade her to go home with them. Since she was so determined to stay in her apartment, Marty told her, "Mother, the doctor gave orders you can no longer live there, and as I see it, you have three choices. You can remain here in the hospital, go to a nursing home, or come home with Leola and me. We have a room for you, and we'd like for you to come home with us. You will be well looked after. You know that."

Mother chose the only alternative acceptable to her, and that was to go home with Marty and Leola to Burlington. About six weeks later, she passed away with cardiac failure, on March 18, 1977, at the age of 79. She had taken heart medication for a number of years.

My mother was a devout Christian, and always demonstrated her faith in her works and deeds. I thank Mother for my faith I acquired through her teachings, and for taking me to church and Sunday school when it was not easy to do. My faith has guided me and given me strength and courage in all situations. I have received many blessings along life's way.

Pamela and Ken parted after twelve years of marriage. After Pamela found a place to live in the vicinity of the University of New Mexico, Ken moved to the same area to make it easier for Brian and Joy to be near each parent. There was also a good school nearby for the children to attend.

Pamela attended the University of New Mexico and received an M.S. degree in communications. She left nursing and worked in public relations for the New Mexico Power Co. for a few years. Then she decided to go back to nursing and attended the University of New Mexico and earned an M.S. degree in psychiatric nursing and became a clinical nurse specialist in that field. She was also a firm believer in alternative healing and took training at the Colorado Center of Healing Touch to become a healing touch practitioner. She became active as a teacher in that field and taught classes in different cities all over the U.S.

Today Pamela writes articles for a column in the *New Mexico Nurses Association Paper* called *"Nurses Notes."* The paper is published bimonthly. She also struggled to have her own business called the New Mexico Therapeutic Nursing Center. She ended up supporting the business instead of it supporting her, and she had to give it up.

Through nursing meetings she attended, Pamela met a special person, Aron Skyrpeck, who was in the same field of nursing she was in. Their friendship grew, and later, Aron was offered a scholarship at the Yale University School of Nursing in New Haven, Connecticut to study for his master's degree in psychiatry. Upon graduating with honors, he returned to Albuquerque, and their friendship continued to grow. They developed a working relationship and a close personal one. Early in the year of 1999, Aron was offered a teaching job at Yale University. As he discussed this with Yale personnel, he asked what opportunities they might have for Pamela. Miracle of miracles, through Aron, Pamela was offered a full scholarship to attend Yale University to study for her Ph.D. in psychiatric nursing. She had not planned on continuing her education and feels this is a special gift. They moved to New Haven, quite an adventure. Aron decided not to accept the teaching position but acquired a job at one of the hospitals in his nursing field. They are now in the process of getting settled and are happy with their move.

GOLDEN YEARS

Chapter 10

WHEN I RETIRED FROM HIRAM WALKERS at the age of 65, I received a nice pension and insurance benefits. While employed there, I was able to pay off the mortgage on my home that I had purchased after my divorce. In 1976, Pam and Ken moved to New Mexico, and I replaced my 10-year-old Rambler with their small hatchback Rambler. In 1979, I purchased a new Thunderbird that I drove for 10 years. I might still have it, except automobiles were being developed which could travel many more miles on a gallon of gas and the T-Bird got very poor gas mileage. Now I have a Mercury Marquis that is a very comfortable car and a pleasure to drive. Hiram Walkers was a very nice place to work. The work was interesting and quite diversified. They sent me to various seminars and to Bradley University for a course to become a licensed audiometric technician which qualified me to give hearing tests required by OSHA.

In January, a month after I retired from Hiram Walkers and had just returned from a trip to New Mexico to visit my children, I received a phone call from a gentleman named Arthur Warsaw. He lived in Colfax, Illinois, and was someone I had met about eight years before. He still had my phone number and decided to find out what I was doing. He asked me for a dinner date which I accepted, and we continued to date. We were married that fall on November 26, 1982. This was another "one of the best decisions" I made. We have had 17 happy years together and are hoping for 25.

We had been living in my home, and after we were married seven years, we realized we needed more space as Art is a very active person. Since Art felt more like a guest there, we decided to build a new home. After we completed our new home and moved, Art felt more at home with the large basement he made into an office for his file cabinets and large drawing board, and now has space to work when he wants to.

Our new home is equipped with all the available appliances. Our refrigerator has an icemaker with cold water and ice dispensed through the door of the freezer side, and the kitchen cupboards have pull-out shelves in the lower units (what a blessing in my older years). We also have an in-house vacuum cleaning system where the dirt is collected into a container in the basement which Art empties and then cleans the filter a couple times a year.

Five years ago, we purchased a computer that has kept me occupied learning to use it. It certainly has a mind of its own and won't let me do things the way I want to; it makes me conform to its rules. I read in the *Family Circus*, "When the computer fights back, it's a disputer." That is an apt description of the way I feel about it.

Art was born in Anchor, Illinois, the fifth child of 10 children. He graduated from high school at the age of 16, as he had completed two grades in one year. One of his older brothers worked for Caterpillar Tractor Co., and after Art graduated from high school, he encouraged Art to apply for admission into their four-year apprentice machinist school and was accepted. Art was given extra training in their drafting program, and after graduation, he continued to work for the company. He was soon promoted to line foreman, one of the youngest ever appointed to that position. He continued to work for Caterpillar until he was drafted into the Air Force the last year of World War II and was sent to the Philippines and Japanese area of conflict.

After the war ended and he was discharged, Art returned to Caterpillar but soon became restless after seeing so much of the world. His father had a dealership for International Harvester farm machinery, and Art applied for and received a dealership in the small town of Minier, Illinois. While selling tractors and tractor parts to the farmers in that area, Art listened to their complaints that the tractors needed more versatility to have more speeds. He designed and patented a nine-speed transmission for the IH tractors, something no one else believed could be done, and went into business with a partner, producing *"nine-speed kits"* for the tractors. This was a very important invention since it was the start of the advance design of machinery used in farming today.

After five years, Art sold his half of the company and formed an independent company. He created a business in Colfax, Illinois, manufacturing power-testing equipment, called a dynamometer, for which he made many designs and has acquired many patents over the years. He designed, produced, and sold Dynamometers for testing the power and torque of any size motor. His oldest son took over the manufacturing business, but Art retained the sales division, and he has continued to be the designing engineer for the company. Art is still active in that capacity. We have done a lot of traveling for the business all over the United States, Canada, Mexico, the

Netherlands, Germany, Switzerland, and France. I have seen a lot more of the world than I ever expected to.

We spent several winters in a resort area in southwestern Texas just west of Big Bend National Park. We met many nice, friendly people there. Art enjoyed the tennis courts, and I spent many days on the golf course. We liked to hike in the mountains, and sometimes Art planned a day of hiking with other hikers, but they hiked much higher and farther than I cared to go. When he and I hiked alone, Art always helped me over the real steep and difficult places. For a couple of years upon leaving that area in the spring, we traveled farther west to Phoenix, Arizona, to visit some of our friends there and Art's daughter and granddaughter, Julie and Whitney. One winter we went on to Prescott Valley, Arizona, to see my granddaughter, Cheri. She is a veterinarian and is employed at an animal clinic there. After leaving Cheri's, we continued on to Albuquerque and Los Alamos to visit other members of my family. When Ben, my first great-grandchild, was a year and a half, Darlene and I flew to California for a three-day visit. I enjoyed reading and playing with Ben and seeing his mother and dad, Kristin and Neal.

We don't travel as much anymore, but we are comfortable and enjoy our nice home. Ever since my two sons planned and ordered a computer[12] suitable for us to purchase, I have spent many hours on it with different projects—my biggest accomplishment will be this book. Art is still busy on the drawing board designing new applications for his business. He has four children, three sons who live in Illinois, and a daughter and

granddaughter who live in Arizona. Art has three granddaughters and one grandson.

Art took dancing lessons, so we could enjoy that activity together. We go to many dances all over this area and to the Quadrant Club. It is not classified as a singles group anymore, and all people are welcome there now. Art enjoys tennis and belongs to a seniors' group, and they play three times a week, weather permitting. I learned to play golf after my divorce, and Art plays some, but it's not his favorite game. I belong to a couple of golf leagues, which keeps me very active. I have also helped my children with many of their projects over the years.

Now when they ask me to help them with a project, I say, "Okay, if it is nothing physical. I am too old and decrepit for that."

They reply, "Oh, Mom, you're only old and decrepit when you want to be."

After Cliff and Cheryl had been married 18 years, Cliff informed Cheryl he didn't want to be married anymore and wanted a divorce. This devastated Cheryl, but she worked through her grief and decided to go back to college part-time since she already had a full-time nursing job. Her desire was to obtain her B.S. in nursing. She studied very hard and graduated Summa Cum Laude. Then she decided to go on for her master's degree to be a nurse practitioner. With many hours of study, she also accomplished that and is now working for a doctor specializing in geriatrics which is the field Cheryl is interested in. After her divorce, Cheryl began dating a man, Bruce Wiemer, of Delavan, Illinois, who is afflicted with Muscular Dystrophy. He had this from childhood, but he was determined to have a life and not give in to it. He graduated from the University of Illinois and obtained his CPA (certified public accountant) license to enable him to earn his livelihood. Five years ago, they married and built a home about two miles from us. I'm so happy they are near, enabling our families to spend more time together. Bruce is a very kind, loving person with a good sense of humor, and we love and enjoy him very much.

MY GRANDCHILDREN

Chapter 11

KRISTIN MARIE POTTER, a beautiful young lady born July 16, 1967, has always been creative and quite artistic. One summer when we visited them, Kristin was about seven or eight, and she liked to put on plays for us. She designed the stage in the front of their condo and wrote a scenario for the children to take part in, including herself. She was always a very active person, and even had a paper route which she received an award for being one of the best paper delivery persons.

When she was a little older, Kristin asked me to teach her to sew, because she had a pillow project. She had some beautiful brocade material she thought would make nice pillows for all of them to enjoy. On my next visit, she had them all finished and they were very pretty and serviceable. Kristin enjoys being creative and learning something new. For their home, she has used many creative ideas in the décor. She enjoys crafts and has made some beautiful articles for her mother.

In school, Kristin entered the science contest, rated very high with her projects, won ribbons and went on to the state competition with them. In 1989 Kristin graduated from New Mexico State University with a B.S. in electrical engineering. That summer she began working at the lab in Los Alamos and met another engineer, Neal Pederson, on a bus going to Santa Fe to a function they were both attending for the lab. The following year, on November 28, 1990, Neal became my grandson-in-law. They both obtained jobs in the San Francisco, California area and worked there about five years. While there, Neal earned his master's degree in electrical engineering. On November 15, 1993, they had a precious boy, Benjamin James, my first great-grandchild.

In 1996, they moved back to Los Alamos where Neal is self-employed as a consultant in computer engineering. They lived in the condo where Kristin lived until she was about 11. Jim and Darlene had purchased it from the lab just before Jim went back to college to work on his Ph.D. After moving back to Los Alamos, Kris and Neal had a beautiful little girl, Michelle Nicole, on January 13, 1997, blessing me with my third great-grandchild.

This past summer they built a new home in Los Alamos, moving into it on August 15, 1998, and Kristin is a stay-at-home Mom. Jim and Darlene enjoy having their grandchildren near them, and they keep me posted about the cute and clever things they do and say (which are many, Cheryl says, but she is jealous because her two grandchildren live so far away from her)!

John Scott Potter is a very intelligent and well-educated young man, born on October 26, 1967. Jim and Darlene took him from a foster care home for adoption when he was nine months old—a darling happy baby. John was quite a serious, studious little boy when he was growing up, and his favorite thing to do was read. For Christmas or his birthday, he always wanted books. He enjoyed all sports and especially enjoyed the activities available in the area where he lived. He loved fishing, hiking, and camping in the mountains with his friends. He was active in scouts and earned the rank of Eagle Scout while in high school. John enjoyed basketball in high school and received a basketball scholarship to the Lewis and Clark College in Portland, Oregon. The college had an overseas program for students to go to different countries to study for six months. John was one of 25 students chosen for one of the college-study programs. That year, the group went to Nepal for six months, and John lived with a Nepali family. One of the interesting events he experienced was a trek from the southern border of Nepal, all the way across the country to the northern border of Nepal, to the Himalayan Mountains and Mt. Everett. After graduating in 1988, he worked a year, then enrolled at the University of California in Santa Cruz to continue his education. He graduated from the University of California with a Ph.D in social psychology in 1994.

John received an appointment to teach at Howard University in Washington DC. He studied to be a writer and has taken a leave from the university to pursue writing and give lectures. Sometime after John moved to Washington, D.C. he changed his name to Jordan Jaiya John.

About three years ago, John located his birth father in Florida and made arrangements to visit him and meet the rest of the family. He has enjoyed being able to get acquainted with his extended family. John has a little daughter, born July 29, 1998, named Jordan Elizabeth whom I am anxious to meet. So now I have five great-grandchildren. We don't travel as much as we have in the past, so I don't know when I'll get to see her. John has promised me pictures.

Gregory James Potter, was born November 13, 1968, in Clovis, New Mexico. Jim and Darlene took him from a foster home at the age of four months for adoption. Greg has a very friendly outgoing personality and is a very caring individual. While in grade school, he took part in the numerous plays put on by the school and was active in sports.

When he was in grade school, Greg was a fast runner, and most usually came in first in the races held in Los Alamos in the summer. Greg has asthma, and this has curtailed his activity in some sports. He is an excellent swimmer and worked at the pool every summer while in high school and was appointed manager of the pool for several seasons.

While in high school, Greg, too, achieved the rank of Eagle Scout and was on the football team. He attended college for two years and moved to Albuquerque to work. He is a very busy, hard-working young man. At the present time, Greg has moved back to Los Alamos, and he is working for his dad in his dad's machine shop

Anna Louise Potter, another beautiful granddaughter, was born May 6, 1974, in Los Alamos, New Mexico. Her family came to Peoria at least two times a year, and we always went to Los Alamos once a year which enabled us to see the children often while they were little, even though we lived so far apart. It was such a joy to be able to be a part of their lives.

Anna was the fourth child and the older children were so always busy with their different activities, I wanted to plan something special for her. On one of their visits to Peoria when Anna was about three years old, I asked her if she would like to attend a special stage-show featuring Mickey Mouse that happened to be in Peoria for that week end. Anna said she would like to go, but because she was so young and a little shy, her mother thought she would back out at the last minute, but she didn't. Her Aunt Cheryl and cousin Johanna, almost two years old, went with us. I felt special that Anna would go with me, and she had such a good time; she loved all the animated animals in the show.

As Anna grew, she participated in the races held in Los Alamos for the school children, winning some of them. At the pool they belonged to, she became an expert swimmer, and all through high school, won a wall full of blue ribbons in competitions. Anna had so many sweatshirts featuring the many events she took part in, she cut all the designs from them, sewed them onto a sheet, and made a comforter with them. What a wonderful keepsake.

Anna worked at the pool as a lifeguard, and after graduating from high school, managed the pool for several summers. She received a scholarship for swimming at the University of South Dakota, but only attended there her freshman year. You can imagine going from the milder winters of Los Alamos to the cold frigid winters of South Dakota—Brrrrrrr.

Anna is active in many sports. She enjoys golf and the hunting games in which the participants wear camouflage clothing and hunt other players, attempting to shoot and hit them with dart balls of paint. She worked at the Civic Pool in Los Alamos while continuing to go to the University of New Mexico branch in Los Alamos. She is now attending New Mexico State University at Los Cruces majoring in computer science and will graduate this May (year 2000.)

Rudolph Harold Potter, born March 7, 1978, in Los Alamos, New Mexico, is another precious grandson. Rudy, as he has always been called, was a very active boy, had roles in various plays at school and was also a winner in many of the community summer races. They were all fast runners. I guess that's why they were so hard to keep up with. On one of my visits there, I was fortunate to be able to attend a school play in which Rudy portrayed a rabbit. He certainly was cute, played his part well, and was a true joy to watch.

In grade school and high school, Rudy was always interested in science and made many experimental toys at home. He entered and placed in many scientific competitions. Sometimes his projects were too advanced for the judges to understand them. He is also a *"Whiz"* with computers and has helped me on many occasions. One summer, Rudy spent a couple of months in Germany at the home of a friend of his dad's. Rudy worked at a computer store in Los Alamos in the summers and on weekends during high school.

Rudy is studying physics at the university in Denton, Texas. Jim has his own consulting business (JPAW, James Potter Accelerator Works) and is consulting in Denton, Texas part-time on the accelerator part of a project for a company which purchased that segment of the Super-Collider to build hospital equipment. Rudy has been working part-time with his dad on this project. Jim rented an apartment in Denton to have a place to live when he is there and shares it with Rudy. Rudy has been kidded about having an older man for a roommate.

Kenneth Douglas Potter, a cute little blonde-headed boy, was born July 2,1968. He enjoyed building all kind of designs with his Legos and also loved his Tonka Trucks. Jerry and Sue decided to purchase Jerry's grandmother Koss's 1955 Chevrolet when Ken was four years old. Ken and his dad flew to Peoria for a visit, then I took them to Keokuk to get the car which they drove back to Los Alamos. He felt so grown up making that trip with his dad. Ken's hobby is mountain biking, and Jerry also likes to mountain bike. They biked together all over the Los Alamos area, and in the summer of 1993, took a five-day *off-road mountain biking* trip from the Silverton, Colorado area to Moab, Utah. Cabins supplied with food and for overnight lodging were provided for the bikers on their way to Utah. They were met at Moab by the trip sponsors and transported in a motor vehicle back to Los Alamos.

   After graduating from high school, Ken entered the Wyoming Technical Institute to become an automotive technician and graduated with honors in 1987. After working over two years in that capacity, he decided he wanted to go to New Mexico State University to study mechanical engineering. He had a good background for that already and entered college at mid-term. Beginning with his fall term, he received a Regents scholarship for the remainder of his schooling. He received his B.S .degree with honors in May 1994, and enrolled that fall in Colorado State University, majoring in Robotics. He graduated with a 4.0 average, earning his master's degree in mechanical engineering in 1996. He is now employed in Albuquerque at Applied Research Association.

   Ken married a darling girl, Karen M. Lewis, from Edgewood, New Mexico, on December 8, 1998, after her graduation from New Mexico State University. She majored in English and earned a degree to teach junior high school. Karen has a position teaching seventh grade in an Albuquerque school at the present time.

   Their hobby is fish, and they have them displayed in beautiful tanks, one of which Ken built of wood and lined with marine epoxy. They have recently purchased their first home and are enjoying being homeowners with their two cats.

Cheri Lynn Potter, a pretty little blonde girl, born May 19,1970, who enjoys sewing, embroidery, and counted cross stitching, has made many beautiful articles. She started by making gifts for her grandmothers for Christmas when she was small. One year, she was into weaving and made us each a little cup mat on her little loom. She wove potholders for us and made us a nice sofa pillow I still use.

Jerry and Sue enjoyed training dogs and taking them to obedience trials, and winning many awards. This exposed Cheri to animals. Cheri's love for animals grew, and she developed a desire to be a veterinarian. When she was old enough, she worked summers for a local vet. After high school, she received a Regents scholarship, and entered the biology program at New Mexico State University to become a veterinarian, graduating with honors. She continued her schooling at Colorado State University in their veterinarian department and graduated Cum Laude in 1996 with a DDV. degree.

She is now employed at a vet clinic in Prescott Valley, Arizona, and recently bought a home there. She has a Sheltie, a Border Collie, and a cat. Someone had abandoned the cat at the animal clinic, and it adopted Cheri. She has friends she enjoys hiking in the mountains with and hiked into the Grand Canyon one weekend. One of Cheri's school friends married after her graduation from college and moved to Alaska. Cheri was invited to their home, and after her visit there, she has used many eloquent adjectives describing the beauty of that state.

As we live in a very mobile society, it is difficult to keep up with family.
Cheri is family-oriented and decided she wanted to be closer to her family if she could locate a position in New Mexico. Cheri has just now acquired a position in a clinic

in Albuquerque, and with the help of her family has moved there.

Dale Allen Richter, born March 2, 1965 in Peoria, was my only grandchild living in this area. So I was able to have more contact with him when he was little. While Cheryl was going to college for nurse's training, she lived in an apartment in Peoria and worked 20 hours a week at Bergner's Department Store in the alteration department. She found a nursery school for Dale during the week, and he stayed with me on Saturdays since I didn't work on weekends. I enjoyed having Dale as he was well- behaved and fun to have around. One nice windy day, Dale brought his kite to fly. The string was very tangled, and I had the task of freeing the string of snarls and rewrapping it, so Dale could fly his kite. It was a difficult job to untangle the string, and I asked him to be careful not to tangle it next time. He had great fun with his kite, getting it way up in the air. After flying it for a long time, he decided to bring the kite down. As I watched him in the back yard, I saw him walking from one side of the lawn to the other repetitively. I asked him why he was doing that, and he told me he was keeping the string from getting tangled.

Dale was very innovative and enjoyed making many things with his Lego building blocks. I kept the Legos, and all of the grandchildren enjoyed playing with them when they visited me. When Allen and Jenni are older, I shall give the set back to Dale for them.

As Dale grew, he played football in high school, and after graduation, entered Illinois Southern University to become an electrical engineer. After his freshman year, his uncle Jim encouraged Dale to apply for a summer job at the lab at Los Alamos. They had a policy of hiring college students during the summer. That's all it took for

Dale to fall in love with the Rocky Mountains. He went to school part-time for a couple of years at the University of New Mexico and then enrolled at the State University of Arizona to get his B.S. degree. They had a special curriculum in Lidar which was his forte.

After graduation, Dale continued there for his M.S. degree, and in the summers, worked at the Los Alamos Lab. In Los Alamos, he met a beautiful and talented girl, Catherine McCabe, who was studying computer science at New Mexico State University. The summer of 1994, following their graduations, they were married in Los Alamos and moved to Virginia . They lived there for three years with Dale working for NASA and Catherine employed by the University of Virginia. On February 28, 1996, Catherine and Dale had a beautiful baby boy; I was blessed with my second great-grandchild, Allen James. Heidi and I made a trip that summer to visit them and meet Allen James.

After living in the east, they began to long for the mountains of New Mexico, and Dale applied for and obtained a position in Albuquerque. After moving to Albuquerque in February, they had a darling little girl named Jennifer Marie, born June 12, 1997, my fourth great-grandchild. They had a home built on the east side of the Sandia Mountain, and Catherine is a stay-at-home mother.

Bert James Richter was born in Swan River, Manitoba, Canada, on December 29, 1965. At the age of nine, after being in several foster homes, he was placed with the Lutheran adoption agency. Cheryl and Cliff applied for his adoption, and in December 1975 with Dale, they drove to Canada to bring him to Illinois. He was a cute little red-headed boy, rather undersized for his age. I think he certainly was a brave little boy to come to another country with strange people, but he seemed to thrive and grew into a very nice young man with many abilities.

      After he graduated from high school, he applied to the Police Department of Illinois to become a policeman. Because of his age, he was not accepted. He enlisted in the U.S. Army, and after basic training, he was placed in the medic department and discovered he liked that kind of work. He was stationed in Germany for a period of a year. Upon returning to the U.S. and finishing his term of enlistment, with the aid of his parents, he went to a paramedic school in Boston, Massachusetts; one of the best schools in the U.S. Upon graduating, he found a place of employment at the Paramedic Facility in Bloomington, and Champaigne, Illinois, working there eight years. At that time the ownership of the facility change, and Bert felt the need to change his profession. He read an ad in the paper for police trainees wanted. He applied, and with his resume, had no difficulty in being accepted. He attended the Illinois Police Academy in Champaign for the required curriculum, graduated with honors in September of 1998, and has a position with the police department in Rantoul, Illinois.

      Johanna Marie Richter was born July 27, 1977, in Peoria, Illinois. She was certainly *Queen of her castle,* with two older brothers to dote on her and the *"apple"* of my eye. I certainly did my share of doting, too. When Johanna's sister was one and she was three, it was difficult for Cheryl to do her grocery shopping when she took both of them with her. Sometimes I would care for them while Cheryl shopped. One time, Cheryl took Heidi with her to the grocery store, and I took Johanna to the park. The girls always loved the parks. The only slide in the park was rather high, and I let Johanna (she was three years old at the time) climb up and was going to catch her as she came down. The slide had only steps up and no landing at the top, and Johanna stood on the top step on one foot, swinging the other one back and forth, just enjoying looking all around. It was a thrill for her to be up so high, and I had to really plead with her to get her to slide down. When she finally came down, I wouldn't let her go up again, and took her to the swings instead.

While in grade school, Johanna learned to play the piano and the saxophone quite well and marched in school parades. With her sister, she took dancing lessons for several years. She belonged to a Brownie Troop and Girl Scouts, and I bought more than my share of Girl Scout cookies. She is gifted artistically but has only used it for a hobby.

For her first two years of college, Johanna attended the junior college near us and now is in her senior year, majoring in finance at the University of Arizona, the school her brother Dale received his degree from. It is lonesome for her to be so far from home. She has been able to go to Albuquerque to visit Dale and his family occasionally, so that helps her not to be so lonely. Johanna attended a college in Ulm, Germany, as an exchange student this past summer. She will graduate in December of 1999.

Heidi Lynne Richter, born May 7, 1979 in Peoria, Illinois, is another darling granddaughter I am blessed with. She was someone for Johanna to compete with and play with. Cheryl often dressed them alike when they were small. She made beautiful dresses, dancing recital costumes, and special Halloween costumes for them.

When Johanna was in preschool, they had a class picnic in the park in May. Heidi and I were invited to join the group, and one of the little students had a birthday.

As the activity progressed, to celebrate his birthday, his mother hired someone whose specialty was entertaining children. The entertainer played a guitar and was dressed as an alligator. At the end of her songs, she played *"Old McDonald"* for the children to participate in. Each child was asked what animal they wanted to be, including Heidi, who answered she wanted to be a snake. After everyone did their animal imitation, she asked Heidi, "and the snake went?" To everyone's surprise, Heidi said, *"Slither Slither,"* and crawled on the ground to demonstrate.

From early on Heidi loved to sing and act, and took part in all the plays during her grade school and high school years. Art and I attended them all, I think. We were kept very active going to Johanna and Heidi's activities. I mentioned to Art once, "Aren't you glad all of my grandchildren don't live near us, or we'd never have time to do anything else?" He agreed.

They both attended the Concordia Lutheran Grade School in Peoria which was a highly rated school, and every four years, the school with the band and Pom Pom girls were invited to attend and march in the Cherry Tree Parade in Washington, D.C. When Heidi was in the fifth grade and Hanna in the seventh grade, the school, with six bus loads of children and parents, made the trip again. I was also invited, and it was a wonderful week-long trip. We were taken to many areas of importance and given tours of the White House and Arlington Cemetery, a concert by the United States Band, a musical play, and many other things. The climax of the trip was viewing the students as they participated in the big parade.

Hanna and Heidi were in the Pom Pom Drill team for several years. One year their team went to Indianapolis, Indiana, for a school competition. Hanna was in the band formations and Heidi in the Pom Pom group. I was invited to go with them, and we certainly had a fun time.

Heidi was in Brownies and Girl Scouts, besides all the school and church activities. Cheryl found good teachers to give her singing lessons all through school. She was invited to become a member in the adult church choir of the Lutheran Church while still in grade school. She is now in her third year at the University of Illinois, studying music and interested in opera. She has a beautiful voice, and everyone enjoys hearing her sing. We have been privileged to attend some of her recitals in Champaign. She was awarded a scholarship last year for excellence.

Brian Ivor Hughes, was born November 9, 1977, in Albuquerque New Mexico. Brian was always a very bright child and interested in learning. The summer Brian was a year-and-a-half old, he was in the back yard with his mother and dad while they were working in their garden. I was there at the time, and we heard Brian say, "Put back, put back." As we checked to see what he meant, Pamela found he had picked a green apricot off their little tree and had taken a bite from it. When he discovered it was sour and not good to eat yet, he wanted to put it back on the tree.

For several summers, he and his sister spent part of the summer with me. A couple of those summers, we attended a family reunion in northeastern Missouri at the daughter of one of my cousins. They lived on a farm, and they had a big swimming pool all the children and some of the adults enjoyed. It was about a 130 mile trip one way. On the return home, the children were tired, and for something special to do, I encouraged Brian to tell his cute little puzzle jokes that were quite popular at that time. One I remember is, "When the elephant hurt his toe, how did they get him to the animal hospital? In a tow truck." Brian and Joy enjoyed swimming and the water slides that were available in the city in Peoria, but they never cared to play in the parks like Hanna and Heidi did. Brian was interested in karate and the martial arts and took some lessons in Albuquerque. His father played golf, and Brian learned to golf and enjoys playing with his dad.

In high school, Brian was on the debate team and traveled to different competitions, which his team won many of. Brian stated the most important thing he learned while on the team was, "the team approach which stressed that to be successful 'one' did not stand out as the winner but learn how important it is to help each other on the team and to work together and win as a team." In other words teamwork.

After graduation, Brian went to a college in the state of Oregon for one year. He was chosen to be an exchange student to Japan and spent two or three months there, staying with a Japanese family. He waited a year before going on to school since he was not sure in what direction he wanted to go, but this year, he is back in college enrolled at the University of New Mexico in Albuquerque. Last Christmas, Brian was invited to visit a friend in Switzerland, and he was there for about three months. Traveling is such good experience for young people.

Joy Elaine Hughes, the youngest of my beautiful granddaughters, was born August 31, 1979, in Albuquerque, New Mexico. When Joy was four, she came to Peoria with her mother for a visit. Johanna and Heidi each had a dance routine they were scheduled to give in a competition in St. Louis while Pamela and Joy were here. We went to St. Louis on a bus, and I thought Joy would be very tired traveling so much. It was a pleasure to see how much she enjoyed it. She never took her eyes off of the dancers the entire program. After they returned to Albuquerque, Pamela enrolled Joy in dancing. She was very petite, and when she was in a dance recital, she looked like a little fairy princess.

She and her brother, Brian, came to Peoria for a month several summers when they were small. Pamela put them on an airplane to Peoria, and for a fee, they were chaperoned by the airline personnel. It was a very safe way for children to fly when not in the company of an adult. Joy enjoyed our trips to Missouri for the family reunions, but found the way home tiring. It was a long way to go and return in one day.

One summer when Joy was ten, her mother wanted me to teach her to sew. Joy wasn't all that interested in sewing, but she did make herself a skirt. The blouse was tedious and too small, so it didn't get finished. I'm explaining this because, when she was older, she became a beautiful seamstress and is very talented in designing some of her own clothes.

When they were older, Joy and Brian spent some of their summers attending camps. Joy belonged to a soccer team and spent a lot of her time in that activity.

She is very artistic and has done some beautiful work with photography, receiving an award on one of her creations. Joy graduated from high school in three years, but was too young to know exactly what she was interested in to go to college. Next semester, she will attend a junior college in New York state where she is living and will start with the basic studies and decide from there what field to major in.

This probably sounds like a brag chapter, and I guess it is, but as a grandparent, I have a license to brag.

APPENDAGES

I'M ADDING A LIST OF ADAGES (it's usually a homely illustration of a general truth) you all might have fun with, like trying to figure out their meaning, what they are referring to, and comparing notes with each other.

1. A stitch in time saves nine.
2. Birds of a feather flock together.
3. A bird in the hand is worth two in the bush.
4. A man is known by the company he keeps.
5. A watched pot never boils.
6. Waste not, want not.
7. Up a creek without a paddle.
8. Sound as a dollar.
9. Straight as an arrow.
10. Haste makes waste.
11. Poor people have poor ways.
12. It's like the pot calling the kettle black.
13. Hard as a rock.

14. Made with a red hot needle and a blazing thread.
15. Heavy as lead.
16. Slow as molasses in January.
17. Rotten to the core.
18. One bad apple spoils the barrel.
19. You reap what you sow.
20. If you play with fire, you get burnt.
21. Look before you leap.
22. A bad penny always returns.
23. Lazy girl takes long thread.
24. What you don't use, you lose.
25. If wishes were horses, beggars would ride.
26. Beggars can't be choosers.
27. Make your head save your heels.
28. A rolling stone gathers no moss.
29. All that glitters is not gold.
30. Monkey see, monkey do.
31. A bad deed comes home to roost.
32. The proof is in the pudding.

My grandmothers often used sayings like these to illustrate a point.

SUMMARY

THESE ARE MY MEMORIES. No doubt all the people involved will have entirely different memories of the same situation. It would be interesting if each one of my children added his or her memories to the story, writing what was important to him or her, and if each of my grandchildren added theirs also. That would make a great addendum to my story. What fun it would be to have my brothers, nieces, and nephews add to the story. I'll look forward to hearing from all of you—your input and output.

But it could be never-ending. As each generation grows, they could add the many changes in their lifetimes and compare—and share their stories with the future families.

Thanks to all of my family for their words of encouragement and support, by their interest in the project, and their willingness to prod me on. I want to express my appreciation to my editor, Tresa Erickson, for her kindness and help. It has been a rewarding experience—the fact I was able to compile and write it in some chronological order amazes me.

I hope I have accomplished the purpose of this book which was to demonstrate the progress and many inventions that occurred during my lifetime, the equipment made available to improve the quality of living, and the vast advancement of technology making that possible.

Instead of losing our families when they move away, through the many methods of communication and travel, we are able to keep in close contact with them and to see them often.

Marie K. Warsaw

Genealogy

Chapter 13

Descendants of Ethel Marie Koss

```
    1  Ethel Marie Koss         1916 -
..     +Harold Lester Potter    1916 - 1984
.....  2    James Martin Potter          1941 -
            +Darlene Louise Danz          1943 -
            3     Kristin Marie Potter          1967 -
                  +Neal Pederson      1967-
                  4           Benjamin James Pederson 1993 -
                  4           Michele Nicole Pederson    1997 -
            3     Jordan Jaiya John    1967 -
                  4           Jordan Elizabeth McCoy-John 1998 -
            3     Greg Potter          1968 -
            3     Anna Louise Potter 1975 -
            3     Rudolf Harold Potter          1978 -
            3     Infant Potter    1979 - 1979
....  2    Jerry Melvin Potter 1944 -
           +Susan Jeane Balcom          1946 -
           3     Kenneth Douglas Potter    1968 -
           3     Cheri Lynn Potter    1970 -
....  2    Cheryl Marie Potter          1947 -
           +Paul Edward Hammond          1945 -
           3     Dale Allen Hammond Richter 1965 -
                 +Catherine McCabe          1966 -
                 4           Allen James Richter       1996 -
                 4           Jennifer Marie Richter    1997 -
           *2nd Husband of Cheryl Marie Potter:
           +Clifford Lee Richter          1941 -
           3     Dale Allen Hammond Richter1965 -
                 + Catherine McCabe          1966 -
                 4           Allen James Richter       1996 -
                 4           Jennifer Marie Richter    1997 -
```

....	3	Bert James Richter	1965 -
....	3	Johanna Marie Richter	1977 -
....	3	Heidi Lynn Richter	1979 -

.... *3rd Husband of Cheryl Marie Potter:
.... +Bruce B. Wiemer   1936 -
.... 2   Pamela Joy Potter   1951 -
.... +Kenneth Ivor Hughes   1947 -
.... 3   Brian Ivor Hughes   1977 -
.... 3   Joy Elaine Hughes   1979 -
   *2nd Husband of Ethel Marie Koss:
..   +Arthur James Warsaw   1918 -

Pictures of some of our ancestors and family, genealogy material, and charts taken from the work of my brother, Martin E. Koss, are on the following pages.

John Edward Jones & Julia Pipkin
Wedding October 5, 1892

Susan C. Lambert & Larkin Jones
Wedding February 12, 1860

Marie Koss & Harold L. Potter
Wedding March 19, 1939

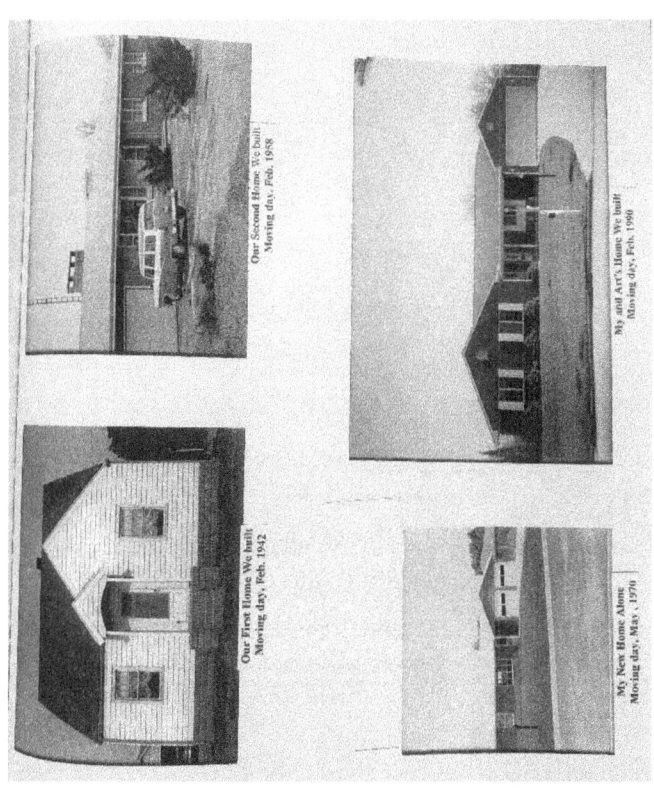

The author and her husband. Marie and Art Warsaw.

Marie, Jim, Jerry, Cheryl, Pamela

The author, Marie K. Warsaw

My brother, Martin E. Koss, has worked with our genealogy for over 50 years. Following is a copy of a paper he sent to me, perhaps some will be interested in it.

Distant cousins of the Queen of England in Kentucky.
By Stratton Hammon

Elizabeth II, Queen of Great Britain, descended from an American. This was Colonel Augustine Warner, born in Warner Hall 3 June 1642 in what is now Gloucester County, Virginia. He died in Virginia 18 June 1681 and during this short life of thirty-nine years sired three daughters:

Mary Warner – the progenitress of Queen Elizabeth II

Mildred Warner – the grandmother of General George Washington.

Elizabeth Warner – the ancestress of hundreds of Virginians and Kentuckians, some of which are listed below.

This remarkable man was the son of Captain Augustine Warner who was a Speaker of the Virginia House of Burgesses and was descended from Edward III, king of England.* Warner Hall, where the son was born, was on the Severn River in what was then York Co., now Gloucester. He was educated in England and also became a Speaker of the Virginia House of Burgesses** and a member of the Honorable Council of the Colony of Virginia.

He married Mildred Reade whose own illustrious lineage is given below, and sired, among others, the three daughters that are the subject of this article.

The descent to Queen Elizabeth II happened in this manner:

Colonel Augustine Warner married Mildred Reade and had daughter:

1. Mary Warner, born about 1666 in then York Co., Virginia, married John Smith and had daughter:

2. Mildred Smith, born 1682, married Robert Porteus (. 1670, d. 1758) and had son:

3. Robert Porteus, born 1704, married Judith Cockayne (b. 1702, d. 1789) had daughter:

4. Mildred Porteus, born 1744, married Robert Hodgson. Their son:

5. Robert Hodgson was born 1776. He married Mary Tucker. Their daughter:

6. Henrietta Hodgson married Oswald Smith (b. 1794, d. 1863) Their daughter:

7. Frances Smith, who died in 1922, married Claud Bowes, 13th Earl of Strathmore, who was born 1824 and died 1904. Their son:

8. Claud Bowes-Lyon, born 1855 in England, married Nina Bentick (d. 1938.)Their daughter

9. Elizabeth Marguerite Bowes-Lyon, born 1904, is the present Queen Mother having married King George VI of England. Their daughter:

10. Elizabeth II, born 1926, is the present queen.

The descent to General George Washington was a follows:

1. Colonel Augustine Warner married Mildred Reade and had daughter:

2. Mildred Warner, born in the York Co., Virginia married Captain Lawrence Washington (b. Sept, 1659, died 1697/8 Westmoreland Co,. Virginia). He left their daughter, Mildred, 2,500 acres on which Mt. Vernon now stands. Their son:
3. Captain Augustine Washington, b. 1694, d. 1743 married:
1. .Jane Butler and had sons Lawrence, Augustine, Butler and daughter Jane.
2. Mary ball in 1730/1 and had seven children: Elizabeth, John Augustine, Samuel. Charles, Mildred, and George, first president of U.S.

* Americans of Royal Descent, pp 247-253
** The Washington Ancestry by Charles A. Hoppin Privately Printed Greenfield Ohio 1932 Vol. I, p 229

If one strain of Warner bold sustained the families of the Queen of England and that of General George Washington, those of descending from the third Warner daughter have a double dose of this lineage, because cousins married. It happened this way:

1. Colonel Augustine Warner married Mildred Reade and had daughter:
2. Elizabeth Warner, born 1672 in Gloucester Co., Virginia, married her first cousin, Colonel John Lewis, known as Councilor John Lewis, born 1669. They became first cousins in this manner: General Robert Lewis landed in York, County Virginia – from England. His son, John Lewis married Isabelle Warner, sister of Colonel

Augustine Warner. John Lewis and Elizabeth Warner had 14 children (at least 5 were girls) One son:
3. William Lewis, died 1784* Northumberland Co., Virginia intestate. He had at least 2 sons – Warner and Jeremiah – of which we are certain and probably also Aaron, John and Henry, all of whom came to Kentucky in 1787. Aaron Lewis, "Gentleman", was made a trustee of Boonesborough, Kentucky at the same time as Daniel Boone. The son of William Lewis was:
4. Jeremiah Lewis born 1762 in Northumberland Co., Virginia, married Rachel Beecham in that same county in 1784. **Jeremiah and Rachel Lewis moved to Green Co., Kentucky between 1790 and 1795. Their daughter:
5. Nancy Lewis, born about 1792 probably in Northumberland Co., married Morgan Jones 10 July 1809 Green County, Kentucky .+ (The Lewis family still has a large department store on the courthouse square in Greensburg, Kentucky. The other intermarried families of that generation were Davis, Daniel, McFarland, Despain.)

The Reade Line
1. Andrew Reade, Lord of the manor of Linkenholt, Hampshire, England, died 1623. His son:
2. Robert Reade, married Mildred Windebanke, daughter of Sir Thomas Windebanke (Obit. 23 October 1607) OF Haines Hall, Berkkshire, and his wife Frances Dymocke, daughter of Sir Edward Dymocke – "Hereditary champion of England." Mildred Windebanke was also sister of Sir Francis Windebanke, Secretary of State to King Charles I (who was beheaded).++ Robert Reade and Mildred Windebanke had son:
3. Colonel George Reade married Elizabeth Marteau, daughter of Nicholas Marteau, a Huguenot who first took

refuge in Belgium, then sailed for Virginia in the "Francis Bona Venture" several months before the Mayflower left England in 1620. He settled on 1,300 acres on York River near Chesapeake Bay. (On this same land 160 years later his descendant, General Washington, fought and won the battle of Yorktown.) Nicholas Marteau became a Justice of York County, a Burgess in General Assembly of Virginia and captain of militia. He married Jane Berkeley, the widow of Lieutenant Berkeley, soon after the latter's death in 1627. Their daughter, Elizabeth Marteau married Colonel George Reade and had daughter:

4. Mildred Reade who married Colonel Augustine Warner.

* Virginia Wills & Administrations 1632-1800 by Clayton Torrence, p 259
** Virginia Magazine of History & Biography April 1939, Vol. VLVII, No. 2 p 143. This license is not listed in the regular marriage bond books but, fortunately had been noted in the County Clerk's fee books.
+ This marriage is verified, and that of all of her sisters and brothers, in a complicated deed of 1828. See Green County, Kentucky Deed Book 13, p 205. The marriage license book was torn but remaining was "….11, 1809".
++The Reade Record, XVI pp 9-12
(This article taken from: Kentucky Ancestors,Vol.7, No .2)

Ethel Marie Koss Potter Warsaw Ancestors

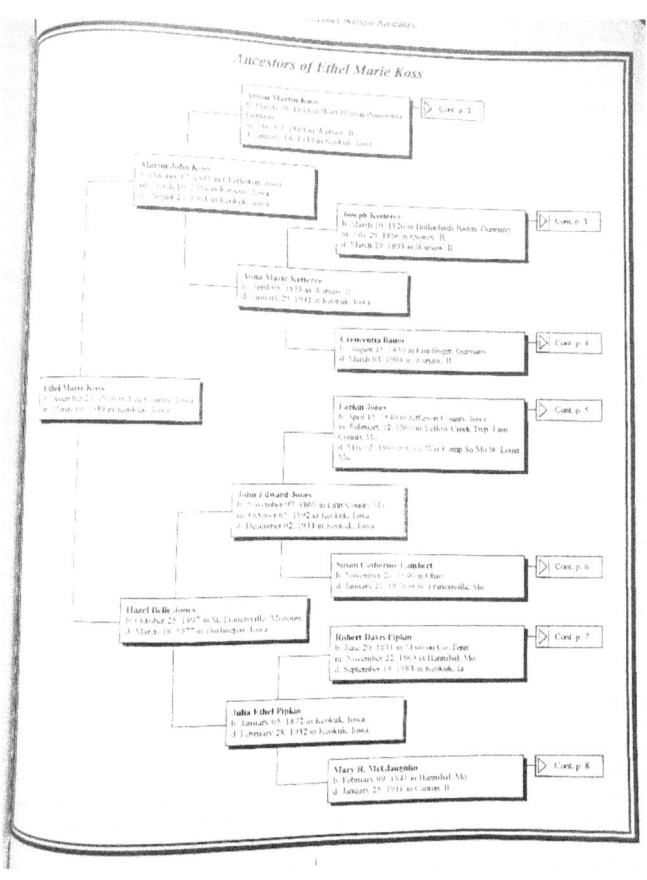

Ethel Marie Koss Potter Warsaw Ancestors

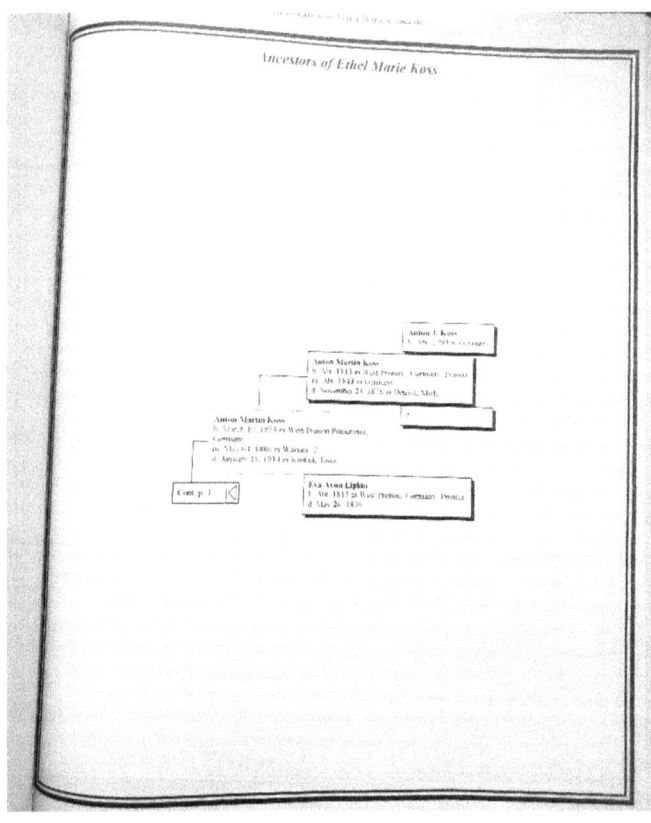

Ethel Marie Koss Potter Warsaw Ancestors

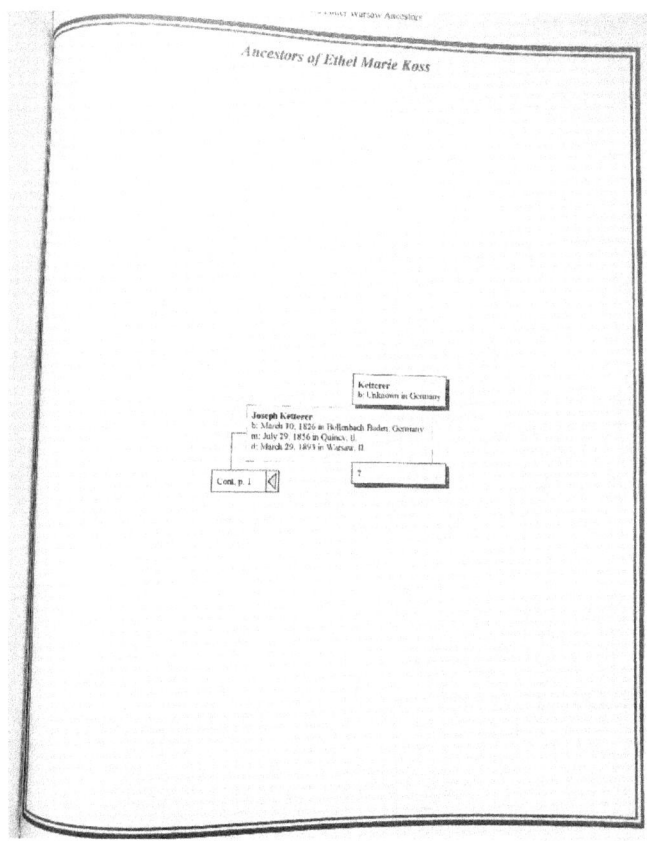

Ethel Marie Koss Potter Warsaw Ancestors

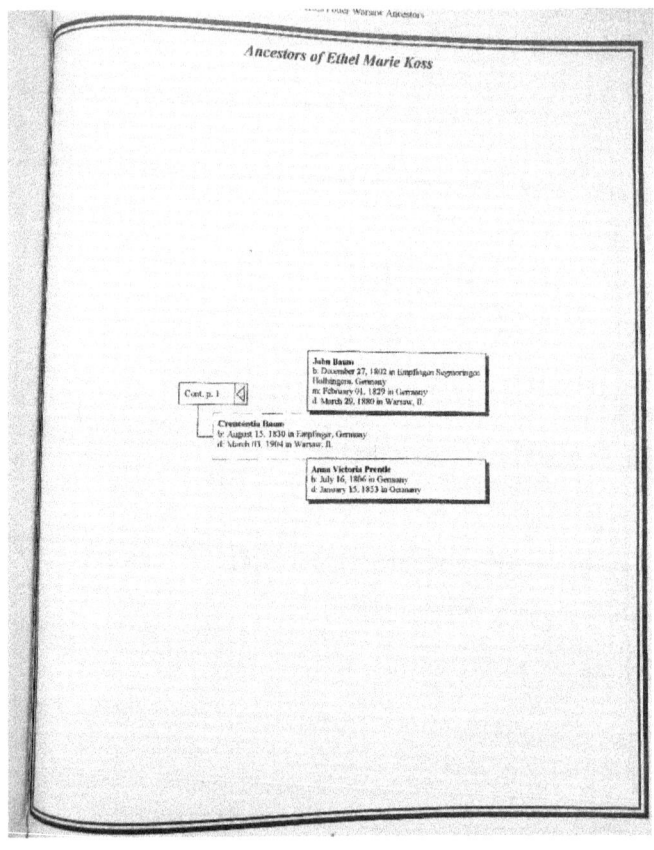

Ethel Marie Koss Potter Warsaw Ancestors

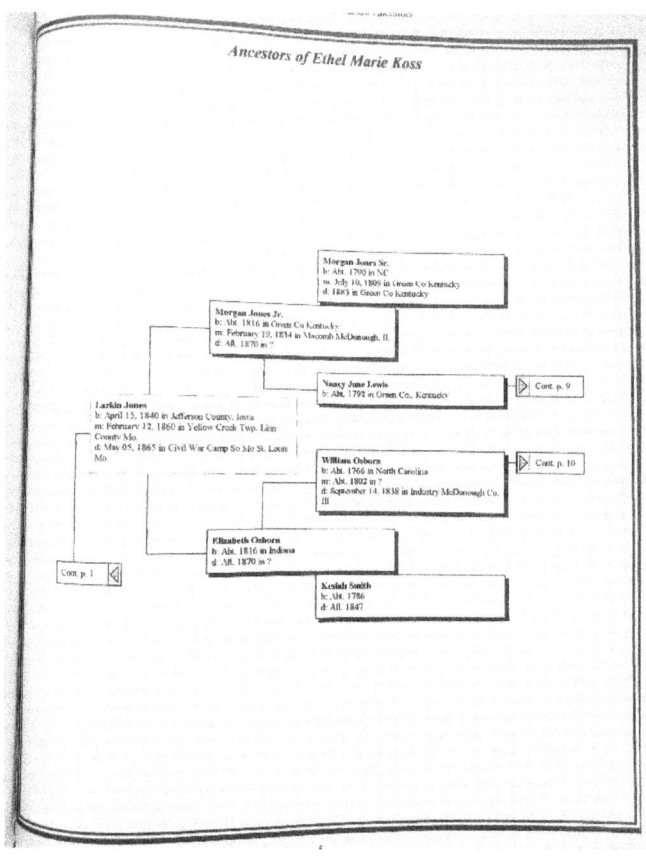

Ethel Marie Koss Potter Warsaw Ancestors

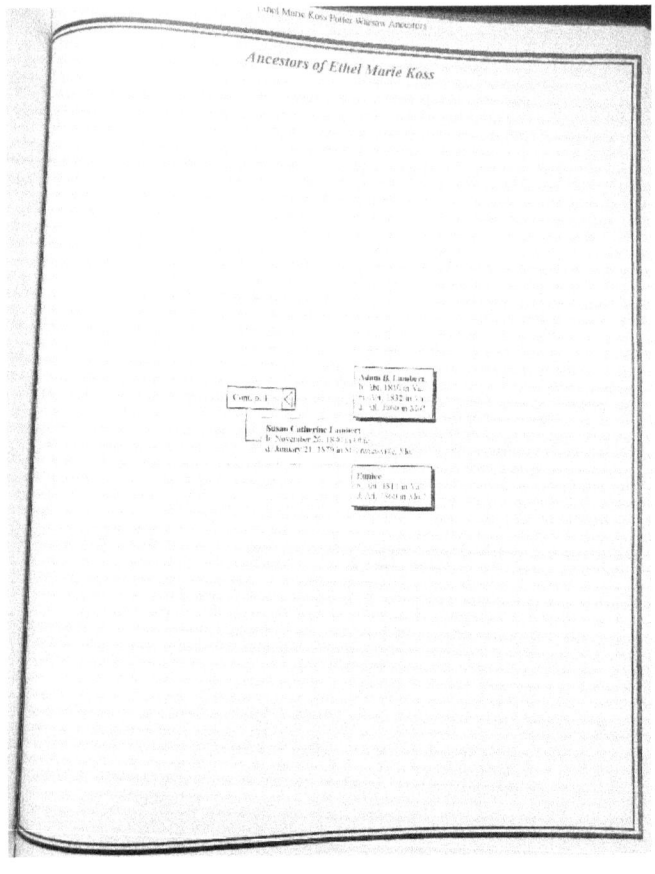

Ethel Marie Koss Potter Warsaw Ancestors

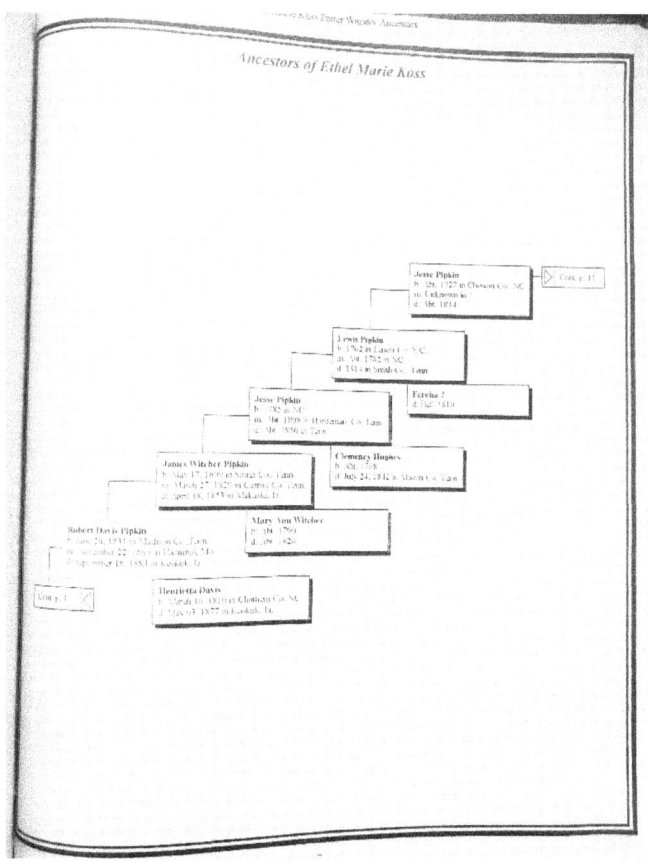

Ethel Marie Koss Potter Warsaw Ancestors

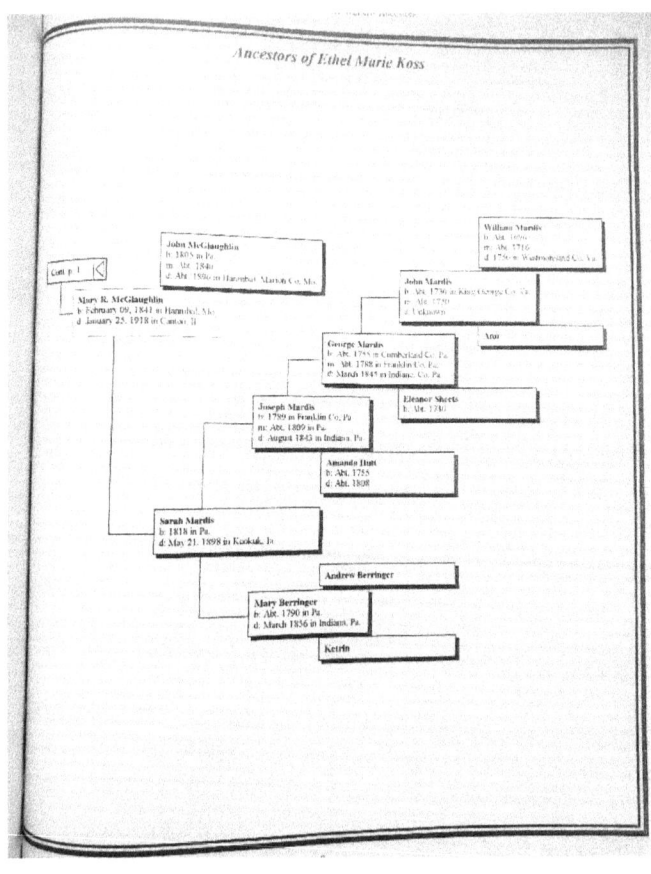

Ethel Marie Koss Potter Warsaw Ancestors

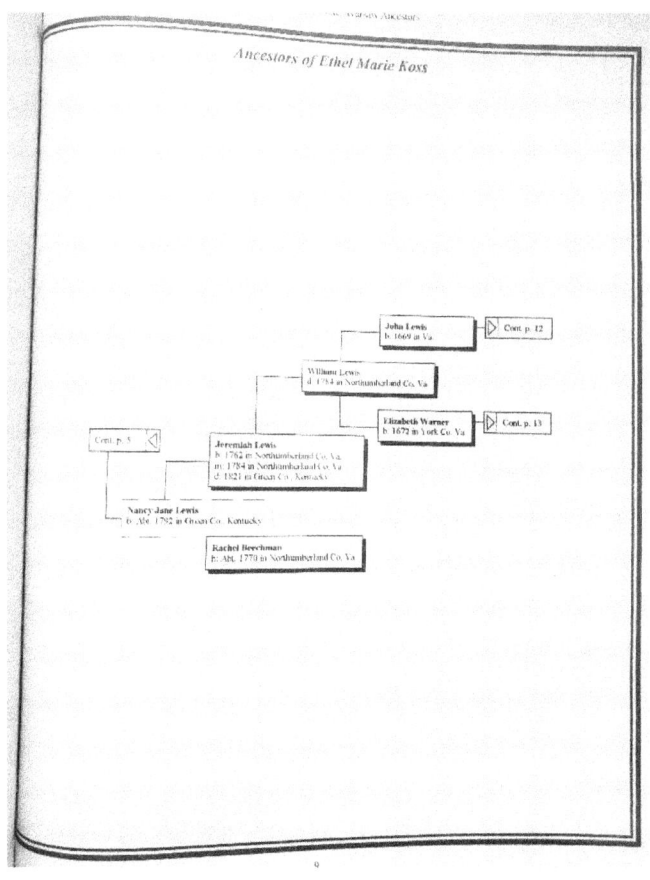

Ethel Marie Koss Potter Warsaw Ancestors

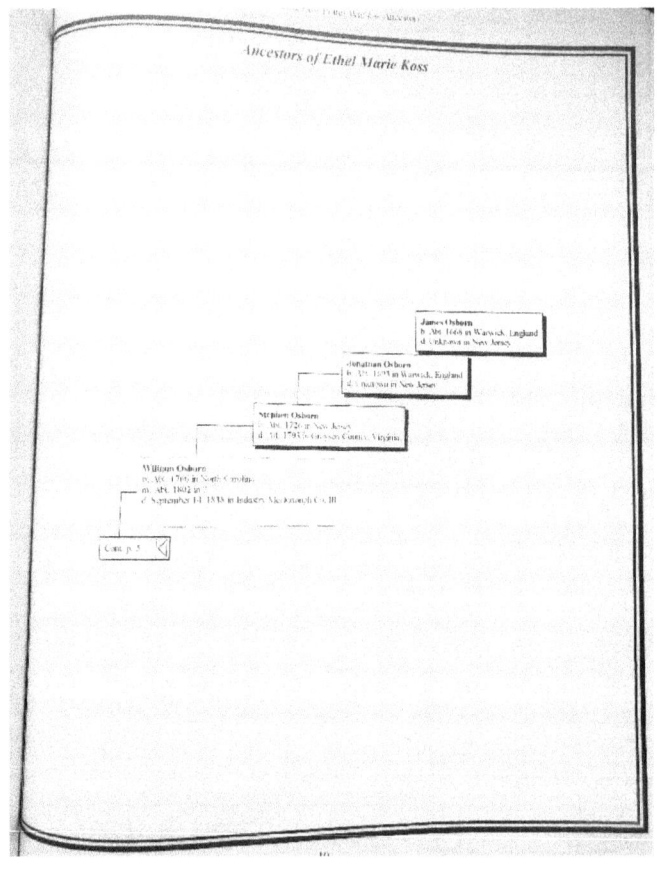

Ethel Marie Koss Potter Warsaw Ancestors

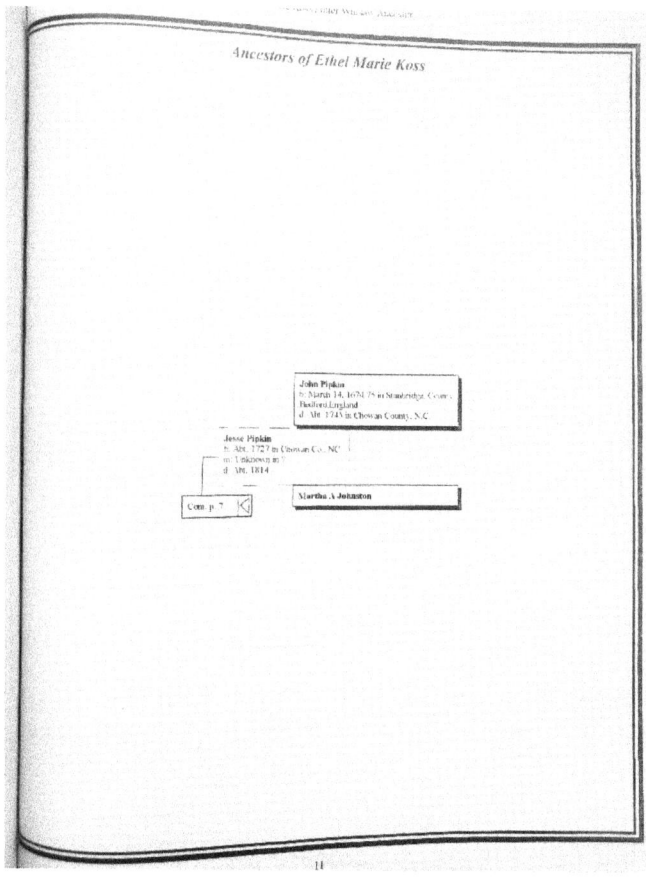

Ethel Marie Koss Potter Warsaw Ancestors

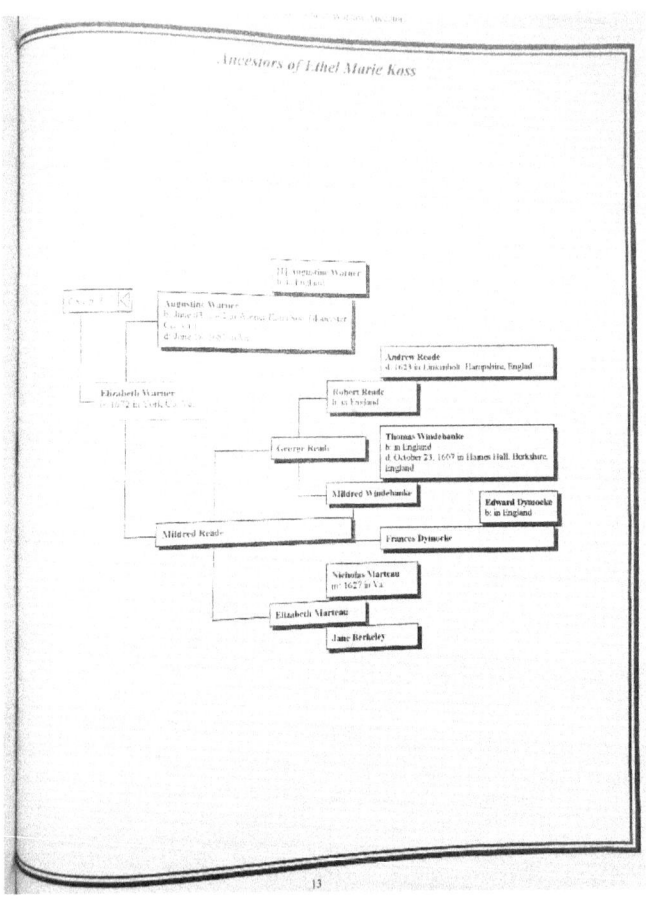

NOTES ON HISTORY AND INVENTIONS

Chapter 14

[1] **Tractors:** The power capability of the modern tractor, which initially replaced only draft animals, has led to higher productivity with a significantly reduced work force. Early agricultural tractors were lumbering, heavy steam-engine vehicles moving on spiked or cleated metal wheels. These were rapidly replaced after the introduction (about 1924) of the general-purpose tractor, which later featured (about 1933) the addition of pneumatic tires with rubber gripping lugs. The engine, in addition to providing traction, or pulling power, also drives a number of power take-off shafts that are used to operate accessory machinery. Any country with advanced agricultural equipment is able to supply enough food for the people of their country and have extra food to export to other countries, thus improving the general economy.

[2] **Detergents:** During World War II, a shortage of fats, from which soap is made, spurred the development of soapless or synthetic detergents. After the war, the need for new types of detergents for automatic washing machines, which were becoming available for home use, accelerated the trend. Detergents developed by treating an aromatic, or benzene-type, compound with sulfuric

acid, then neutralized with alkali to convert the product into a sodium salt. The detergent products were widely used, in the late 1940s and early 50's and proved to be effective in hard, cool, or cold water, whereas soap was often ineffective under such conditions. However, these detergents became a public nuisance because, unlike soaps, they were neither soluble nor biodegradable; that is, once put into water, they tended to remain there, resisting conversion into less complex and more soluble substances. This became a real problem as they created foam in cesspools and in sewage-disposal plants as well. They even appeared in naturally occurring ground and surface waters.

Since these detergents were not soluble nor biodegradable they were replaced by a more desirable formula for our ecology. Replacing the aromatic compound with a so-called linear alkyl-type compound in the process described above led to a more desirable product. It was as effective as the former kind in its detergent action but was more biodegradable and soluble. The new linear alkylate sulfonate was changed to a harmless product by microorganisms in cesspools, sewage-treatment plants, and ordinary soils. Manufacturers of detergents in the U.S. now produce only biodegradable detergent with the changeover being done voluntarily between 1963 and 1965.

[3] **Telephone:** An American inventor, Alexander Graham Bell, produced the first telephone capable of transmitting and receiving human speech in 1887, after having discovered only a steady electric current could be used to transmit speech. In earlier telephones, the current was generated by a battery. In addition to a battery and a transmitter, the local circuit included one

winding of a transformer called an induction coil; the other winding, connected to the line, stepped up the sound wave voltage. As telephone systems grew, manual switching proved too slow and laborious. This resulted in the need to develop a series of mechanical and electronic devices that allowed switching to be done automatically. Now an electronic device transmits either a number of successive impulses of current or a series of audible tones corresponding to the number being called. The electronic equipment at a central switching station automatically translates the signal and routes the call to the receiving party.

[4] **The sewing machine: It** was invented by Elias Howe in 1846, but Isaac Singer developed a more practical sewing machine, and by 1860, was the largest manufacturer of sewing machines in the world. He initiated a number of merchandising practices of major importance, such as installment buying, advertising campaigns, and the provision of service along with sales.

[5]**Airplane:** In 1920, the Wright Brothers, Orville and Wilbur, who for about eight years had worked long and hard on their dream of designing, building, and flying an airplane, finally were able to demonstrate their machine in France. Their demonstration was successful with many people wanting to ride in it. The plane was built with two wings and was called a biplane. Soon after, many people began flying an airplane.

On May 21, 1927, Charles A. Lindbergh made history by flying solo a single- winged airplane from New York to Paris non-stop. Lindbergh named his plane *"The Spirit of St. Louis."* To see this plane, visit the Smithsonian Museum in Washington, D.C. Like the automobile, the development of airplanes is phenomenal. Now we can travel all over the world by jet planes in a very short length of time.

Lighting: Beginning about 1840, a number of incandescent lamps were patented, but none were successful commercially until the American inventor, Thomas Alva Edison, produced his carbon-filament lamp in 1879, his most important invention. His development of a practical electric light bulb and many of his other inventions had a profound effect on the shaping of modern society. Altogether, Edison patented more than 1,000 inventions, but he was more of a technologist than a scientist, adding little to original scientific knowledge. However, in 1883, he did observe the flow of electrons from a heated filament—the so-called Edison effect—whose profound implications for modern electronics were not understood until many years later.

Edison received many honors and awards, including the Congressional Gold Medal in 1928 "for development and application of inventions that have revolutionized civilization in the last century." Edison died in West Orange on October 18, 1931, and I remember what a sad event this was. He was mourned by the entire world.

[7] **Movies:** I'll try to describe a little of how the art of making movies developed. In both the United States and Europe, pictures were drawn by hand and placed in the form of a book. By flipping the pages, the pictures were animated. These were used for amusement in the parlors of the middle class. Much experimentation occurred using a spinning drum to make the pictures appear to come to life. As early as 1852, photographs

began to replace the drawings in the viewing machines. A French physiologist, E J. Marey, made a significant step toward the development of the first motion picture camera. His portable chronophotographe moved a single band of images past an opening at a steady speed, but his filmstrip consisted of oiled paper, which easily buckled and tore. It wasn't until about 40 years later in 1889, that two American inventors, Hannibal Goodwin and George Eastman, developed strips of high-speed emulsion mounted on strong celluloid. This innovation eliminated a major obstacle in more efficient experimentation with moving pictures. Thomas Edison set up a laboratory and is credited with devising the original movie machine. One of his assistants, W.L. Dickson, created the sprocket system, still in use today, by which the film is moved through the camera.

Working at the Edison studio, an American inventor, Edwin S. Porter, produced the first major American film, *The Great Train Robbery* in 1903. This eight-minute movie was hugely successful and is credited with turning movies into a big business. Most all of the European countries began to produce motion pictures, and some of them were very successful. After World War I, motion picture production became a major American industry, generating millions of dollars for the producers. American films became international in character and dominated the world market.

The first practicable sound films were first introduced by Warner Brothers studio in 1926. The process used was known as Vitaphone, the recording of musical and spoken passages on large discs and then synchronized with the action on the screen. These sound films marked the end of the silent era. Unfortunately, the sound and picture were not always in sync and not very satisfying. By 1931, Vitaphone was obsolete, being replaced by the less clumsy, easily adaptable Movietone system. This was a method of recording sound directly on film in a strip alongside the picture. This process was developed by the American inventor, Lee De Forest, and sound films became an international phenomenon almost overnight. The transition from silent to sound films was rapid. Many films released in 1928 and 1929 that were produced as silent pictures were quickly changed by adding sound to them to meet the growing demand. Theater owners rushed to convert their facilities to accommodate sound.

Experimentation with color films began in the early 1900s, but most of the processes developed were disappointing and failed to generate any enthusiasm on the part of the public. By 1933, the Technicolor process, a commercially viable three-color system, had been perfected. The popularity of color grew and was used increasingly throughout the 1940s. In the 1950s, the use of color increased so rapidly it practically eclipsed the black-and-white film.

[8] **History of the emergence of Radio:** Broadcasting evolved from electronic communication through wires, and the roots of broadcasting technology lie in the telegraph using Morse code by American inventor, Samuel Morse, in 1844, and in the invention of the telephone by American inventor, Alexander Graham Bell, in 1876. By 1888, the German physicist, Heinrich Hertz, had demonstrated in the laboratory the existence of radio waves. This discovery attracted the attention of Guglielmo Marconi, an Italian teenager, who later became a physicist and engineer. By 1894, he had sent

Morse code signals up to one mile through the air. The Italian Ministry rejected this invention and deemed it impractical, causing Marconi to go to Great Britain, where investors were highly impressed. Marconi and his colleagues designed most of their products for maritime use, since the critical advantage of the wireless telegraph was in communicating with ships at sea.

On Christmas Eve, 1906 (just ten years before I was born), telegraph operators around the world and at sea were surprised to hear amid the telegraphic codes the sounds of a human voice. Voice communication over radio had been perfected by Canadian-American engineer, Reginald A. Fessenden. His work and the invention of the vacuum tube in 1907 by the American inventor, Lee De Forest, refined the technical basis of radio.

David Sarnoff, an executive of the American Marconi Co., formulated the idea of using radio for broadcasting to mass audiences in 1916, but his superiors were skeptical of Sarnoff's idea and his proposal was shelved. Four years later, an employee at Westinghouse Electric Co., American engineer Frank Conrad, attracted considerable attention when a local newspaper reported on the growing audience listening on crystal radio sets to his evening and weekend amateur broadcast. A local music store provided records to play on the Victrola, and Conrad and his family served as disc jockeys. Conrad was asked by Westinghouse vice president to build a more powerful transmitter in time to announce the outcome of the next U.S. presidential election. In Pittsburgh, Pennsylvania, on November 2, 1920, station KDKA broadcast the announcement that Warren G. Harding had been elected president with about 1,000 people hearing this first news broadcast.

[9] **History of the fountain pen:** A New York insurance agent, Lewis Waterman, patented the first practical fountain pen containing a tube with its own ink reservoir made from a small rubber sack in 1884. He invented a mechanism that, while writing, fed ink from the reservoir to the pen point by capillary action, allowing ink to flow evenly. The fountain pen was the chief writing instrument in the west by the 1920s and remained so until the ballpoint pen was introduced after World War II. The ballpoint pen was developed in the late 1930s and soon became the universal writing tool. The fiber-tip marker was introduced into the U.S. market about 1963 and has challenged the ballpoint as the principal writing tool but has not replaced it.

[10] **Invention of Television:** As the radio industry advanced, inventors were busy working on their next innovation in the electronic revolution—television. The basic elements of an all-electronic television system became available when the American engineer, Philo T. Farnsworth, developed his dissector tube after 1927. In 1928 the first television drama was broadcast on experimental equipment in Schenectady, New York. Throughout the 1930s, research continued to improve the television camera. Their efforts were demonstrated in the dramatic debut of television at the 1939 World's Fair.

The first television sets had small screens about five inches across and transmitted only a black-and-white picture. The age of television had all but dawned in the early 1940s, but World War II intervened, and the attention of industry moved to the war effort. Only six television transmitters continued to broadcast through the war years. After the war, television expanded rapidly until 1948, when about 70 stations were on the air. The FCC, concerned about the limited space available for television transmission in the VHF band (very high frequency, channels 2-13), initiated a four-year freeze on all new licenses in 1948. In 1952, the FCC resumed licensing new stations after it opened the UHF band (ultra high frequency channels 14-83) for television transmission.

After World War II, the popularity of motion pictures began to be challenged by the advent of television. The movie industry responded by developing the Wide Screen, 3-D Movies, and Big-Budget Fantasies, but the popularity of going to the movies steadily declined in the 1950s and 1960s. With movies shown on cable television and the use of VCRs in homes to view rental movies, theater attendance has continued to decline.

[11] **The Space Age:** Practical astronautics commenced with the launching of Sputnik 1 by the Soviet Union in October 1957, and the subsequent formation of the National Aeronautics and Space Administration (NASA) in the U.S. in 1958. Man has always been fascinated by space and the study of the galaxies. Many articles have been written on scientific findings. Despite the scientific foundations laid in earlier ages, space travel did not become possible until the advances of the twentieth century provided the actual means of rocket propulsion, guidance, and control of space vehicles.

In 1957 and 1958, the U.S. and USSR began developing programs to place people in earth orbit. The USSR was first in space with a man in orbit for one hour and 45 minutes on April 12, 1961. The U.S. followed by sending two men into space for 15 minutes on May 5,

1961. After many explorations, the goal of man landing on the moon was accomplished.

Humans achieved the long-awaited goal of actually landing on the moon in 1969. The historic flight of Apollo 11 was launched on July 16. After entering lunar orbit, astronauts Edwin E. Aldrin, Jr., of the Air Force, and Neil A. Armstrong, a civilian who was a Navy veteran, transferred to the lunar module (LM). Lieutenant Colonel Michael Collins of the Air Force remained in lunar orbit following the separation, piloting the command and service module. The LM descended to the surface of the moon on July 20, landing at the edge of *Mare Tranquilitatis*. Armstrong, in his bulky spacesuit descended the ladder a few hours later, and stepped onto the surface of the moon. His first words were, *"That's one small step for a man, one giant leap for mankind."* He was soon joined by Aldrin, and the two astronauts spent more than two hours walking on the lunar surface. They gathered soil samples, took photographs, and set up a solar wind experiment. Armstrong and Aldrin also erected an American flag and talked, by satellite communications, with U.S. president, Richard M. Nixon, in the White House.

Walking and running at one-sixth the gravity of earth they found was not difficult. Returning to the LM and discarding their spacesuits, the two astronauts rested several hours before takeoff. They left the moon by using the lower half of the LM as a launch pad, which remained on the moon. The ascent stage was jettisoned after docking with the command and service module, and the astronauts transferred to the spacecraft. The return flight was without mishap, and Apollo 11 splashed down and was recovered on July 24 in the Pacific Ocean near Hawaii. **By satellite_communication, millions of people watched** live television broadcasts from the moon, (including me). It was a tremendous thrill to watch all of this on TV while it was actually happening.

During the next two decades, more than 1,600 spacecraft of all varieties were launched, mostly in earth orbit. Twelve men walked on the moon's surface and returned to earth.

[12] **The History of** Computers: In the 1880's, an American statistician, Herman Hollerith, conceived the idea of using perforated cards for processing data. By using a system of passing punched cards over electrical contacts, he was able to compile statistical infromation for the 1890 U.S. census. (Earlier in the book, I wrote that Harold, working for ABC manufacturing, was in charge of the payroll department. The method he used was appparently designed from the system described above.)

About the same time, a British mathematician and inventor, Charles Babbage, worked out the principles of the modern digital computer. To many historians, he and his associate, Augusta A. Byron, are considered the true inventors of the modern digital computer, but the technology of their time was not capable of translating their concepts into practice. One of their inventions, however, the analytical engine, had many features of a modern computer. It had an input stream in the form of a deck of punched cards, a "store" for saving data, a "mill" for arithmetic operations, and a printer that made a permanent record.

After World War II, the field of electronics was advancing rapidly and led to the constsruction of the first all-electronic computer in 1946 at the University of Pennsylvania. It was huge, containing 18,000 vacuum tubes, and filling a large temperature and dust controlled room. Its program was wired into the processor and had to be manually altered.

The Age of Computers was beginning. A computer is an electronic device that receives a set to instructions, or program, and performs calculations on numerical data to carry out the program, or compiles and correlates other forms of information. Only by the development of the computer could the modern world of high technology come about. The computer changed manufacturing through the techniques of automation and enhanced modern communication systems, making computers essentioal tools in almost every field of research and applied technology. There are two main types of computers in use today, analog and digital.

In 1948, the transistor was developed at Bell Telephone Laboratories. The transistor is a solid-state device consisting of a tiny piece of semi-conducting material, either germanium or silicon, to which three or more electrical connections are made.

The use of the transistor in computers in late 1950s marked the development of smaller, faster, and more versatile logical elements than were possible with the vacuum-tube machines. Because transistors use so much less power and have a much longer life, this development alone was responsible for the improved machiines called second-generation computers. The componennts became smaller and less expensive to build. During the late 1960s new electronic technique, the integrated circuit , capable of performing the function of 15 to 20 transistors, began to replace the transistor. Then in the mid-1970s, miniaturization and integration techniques made possible the development of the microprocessor which incorporates additional circuitry and memory resulting in smaller computers.

Microprocessors are used in most of today's personal computers.

If you noted the dates and progress in the nineteenth century of some of the inventions I have written about and how slow it was for them to be accepted and produced by the manufactories, you can't help but marvel at how rapid the acceptance and growth of the inventions during the twentieth century has been.

Marie K. Warsaw

Note of Acknowledgement to:
Microsoft Encarta and Funk & Wagnall Encyclopedia